You Can Heal Your Life

Louise L. Hay

Hay House, Inc.
Carson, CA

YOU CAN HEAL YOUR LIFE
by Louise L. Hay

Copyright © 1984, 1987 by Louise L. Hay

Portions of Chapter 15 are from *Heal Your Body* by Louise L. Hay
Revised Edition Copyright © 1982, 1984

The author of this book does not dispense medical advice nor prescribe the use of any technique as a form of treatment for physical or medical problems without the advice of a physician, either directly or indirectly. The intent of the author is only to offer information of a general nature to help you in your quest for physical fitness and good health. In the event you use any of the information in this book for yourself, which is your constitutional right, the author and the publisher assume no responsibility for your actions.

Library of Congress Catalog Number: 88-200391
ISBN: 0-937611-01-8

93 94 95   29 30 31
First Printing, October 1984
Twenty-Eighth Printing, August 1993

Published and distributed in the United States by:

Hay House, Inc.
1154 E. Dominguez St.
P.O. Box 6204
Carson, CA 90749-6204 USA

Printed in the United States of America

Dedication

May this offering help you find the place within where you know your own self-worth, the part of you that is pure love and self-acceptance.

Acknowledgments

I acknowledge with joy and pleasure:

My many students and clients who taught me so much and encouraged me to put my ideas down on paper.

Julie Webster for nurturing me and pushing me in the early stages of the book.

Dave Braun who taught me so much during the editing process.

Charlie Gehrke for being so helpful in creating our New Center, and for providing me the support and time to do this creative work.

Table of Contents

Part 3
Putting These Ideas to Work

Part 4

Foreword

If I were cast away on a desert island and could have only one book with me there, I might well choose Louise L. Hay's, *"You Can Heal Your Life."*

Not only is it the essence of a great teacher, it is also the powerful and very personal statement of a great lady.

Louise shares some of her journey to where she is in her evolvement now in this wonderful new book. I resonated in admiration and in compassion to her story — too briefly sketched here, in my view but, perhaps that's another book.

It's all here is my point. All you need to know about life, its lessons and how to do the work on yourself is right here. And this includes Louise's reference guide to probable mental patterns behind dis-ease, which is truly remarkable and unique — in my experience. A person on a desert island who found this manuscript in a bottle could learn all he or she needs to know to make this life be the one that gets the job done.

Desert island or not, if *you* have found your way to Louise Hay, perhaps even "accidentally," you're well on your way. Louise's books, her remarkable healing tapes and her inspired workshops are wonderful gifts to a troubled world.

It was my own deep investment in working with persons with AIDS that led me to meeting Louise and utilizing concepts from her healing work.

Each AIDS person I worked with and for whom I played Louise's tape, "A Positive Approach to AIDS," *got* Louise's message on the first hearing — and many made playing this tape part of their daily healing ritual. One man named Andrew told me, "I go to bed with Louise, and I get up to her every day!"

My respect and love for Louise grew as I observed my beloved AIDS people make their transitions enriched and at peace and complete — more full of love and forgiveness for themselves and everyone else for having had Louise in their lives — and with a quiet respect for having created that precise learning experience.

I have been gifted in my life with many great teachers, some of them saints, I'm sure, and even avatars, perhaps. Yet Louise is a great teacher one can speak with and be with because of her enormous capacity to listen and to be in unconditional love while sharing doing the dishes. (In the same way another teacher I hold as great makes terrific potato salad.) Louise teaches by example and lives what she teaches.

I am deeply honored to invite you to make this book part of your life. You — and it — are worth it!

DAVE BRAUN

VENTURES IN SELF-FULFILLMENT
DANA POINT, CALIFORNIA
SEPTEMBER 1984

Part 1
INTRODUCTION

Suggestions to My Readers

I have written this book to share with you my readers that which I know and teach. My little blue book *HEAL YOUR BODY* has become widely accepted as an authoritive book on the mental patterns that create diseases in the body.

I have had hundreds of letters from readers asking me to share more of my information. Many persons who have worked with me as private clients, and those who have taken my workshops here and abroad, have requested I take the time to write this book.

I have set up this book to take you through a session, just as I would if you came to me as a private client or attended one of my workshops.

If you will do the exercises progressively as they appear in the book, by the time you have finished, you will have begun to change your life.

I suggest you read through the book once. Then slowly read it again, only this time do each exercise in depth. Give yourself time to work with each one.

If you can, work through the exercises with a friend or with a member of your family.

Each chapter opens with an affirmation. Each of these is good to use when you are working on that area of your life. Take two or three days to study and work with each chapter. Keep saying and writing the affirmation that opens the chapter.

The chapters close with a treatment. This is a flow of positive ideas designed to change consciousness. Read over this treatment several times a day.

I close this book by sharing with you my own story. I know it will show you that no matter where we have come from nor how lowly it was, we can totally change our lives for the better.

Know that when you work with these ideas my loving support is with you.

Some Points
of My Philosophy

We are each 100% responsible for all of our experiences.

Every thought we think is creating our future.

The point of power is always in the present moment.

Everyone suffers from self-hatred and guilt.

The bottom line for everyone is,
"I'm not good enough."

It's only a thought, and a thought can be changed.

Resentment, criticism and guilt
are the most damaging patterns.

Releasing resentment will dissolve even cancer.

When we really love ourselves, everything in our life works.

We must release the past and forgive everyone.

We must be willing to begin to learn to love ourselves.

Self-approval and self-acceptance in the now
are the key to positive changes.

We create every so-called "illness" in our body.

In the infinity of life where I am, all is perfect,
whole and complete, and yet life is ever changing.
There is no beginning and no end,
only a constant cycling and recycling
of substance and experiences.
Life is never stuck or static or stale,
for each moment is ever new and fresh.
I am one with the very Power that created me and this Power
has given me the power to create my own circumstances.
I rejoice in the knowledge that I have the power
of my own mind to use in any way I choose.
Every moment of life is a new beginning point
as we move from the old. This moment is a new point
of beginning for me right here and right now.
All is well in my world.

❤️ Chapter One
WHAT I BELIEVE

"The gateways to wisdom and knowledge
are always open."

**Life is Really Very Simple. What We Give
Out, We Get Back**

What we think about ourselves becomes the truth for us. I believe that everyone, myself included, is 100% responsible for everything in our lives, the best and the worst. Every thought we think is creating our future. Each one of us creates our experiences by our thoughts and our feelings. The thoughts we think and the words we speak create our experiences.

We create the situations, and then we give our power away by blaming the other person for our frustration. No person, no place, and no thing has any power over us, for "we" are the only thinkers in our mind. We create our experiences, our reality and everyone in it. When we create peace and harmony and balance in our minds, we will find it in our lives.

Which of these statements sounds like you?

"People are out to get me."
"Everyone is always helpful."

Each one of these beliefs will create quite different experiences. What we believe about ourselves and about life becomes true for us.

The Universe Totally Supports Us in Every Thought We Choose to Think and Believe

Put another way, our subconscious mind accepts whatever we choose to believe. They both mean that what I believe about myself and about life becomes true for me. What you choose to think about yourself and about life becomes true for you. And we have unlimited choices about what we can think.

When we know this, then it makes sense to choose "Everyone is always helpful," rather than "People are out to get me."

The Universal Power Never Judges or Criticizes Us

It only accepts us at our own value. Then it reflects our beliefs in our lives. If I want to believe that life is lonely and that nobody loves me, then that is what I will find in my world.

However, if I am willing to release that belief and to affirm for myself that "Love is everywhere, and I am loving and lovable," and to hold on to that new affirmation and to repeat it often, then it will become true for me. Now loving people will come into my life, the people already in my life will become more loving to me, and I will find myself easily expressing love to others.

Most of Us Have Foolish Ideas About Who We Are and Many, Many Rigid Rules About How Life Should Be Lived

This is not to condemn us, for each of us is doing the very best we can at this very moment. If we knew better, if we had more understanding and awareness, then we would do it differently. Please don't put yourself down for being where you are. The very fact that you have found this book and have discovered me means that you are ready to make a new positive change in your life. Acknowledge yourself for this. "Men don't cry!" "Women can't handle money!" What limiting ideas to live with.

When We are Very Little, We Learn How to Feel About Ourselves and About Life by the Reactions of the Adults Around Us

It is the way we learn what to think about ourselves and about our world. Now, if you lived with people who were very unhappy, or frightened, guilty, or angry, then you learned a lot of negative things about yourself and about your world.

"I never do anything right." "It's my fault." "If I get angry, I'm a bad person."

Beliefs like this create a frustrating life.

When We Grow Up, We have a Tendency to Recreate the Emotional Environment of Our Early Home Life

This is not good or bad, right or wrong; it is just what we know inside as "home." We also tend to recreate in our personal relationships the relationships we had with our mothers or with our fathers, or what they had between them. Think how often you have had a lover or a boss who was "just like" your mother or father.

We also treat ourselves the way our parents treated us. We scold and punish ourselves in the same way. You can almost hear the words when you listen. We also love and encourage ourselves in the same way, if we were loved and encouraged as children.

"You never do anything right." "It's all your fault." How often have you said this to yourself?

"You are wonderful." "I love you." How often do you tell yourself this?

However, I Would Not Blame Our Parents for This

We are all victims of victims, and they could not possibly have taught us anything they did not know. If your mother did not know how to love herself or your father did not know how to love himself, then it would be impossible for them to teach you to love yourself. They were doing the best they could with what they had been taught as children. If you want to understand your parents more, get them to talk about their own childhood; and if you listen with compassion, you will learn where their fears and rigid patterns come from. Those people who "did all that stuff to you" were just as frightened and scared as you are.

I Believe That We Choose Our Parents

Each one of us decides to incarnate upon this planet at particular points in time and space. We have chosen to come here to learn a particular lesson that will advance us upon our spiritual, evolutionary pathway. We choose our sex, our color, our country, and then we look around for the particular set of parents who will mirror the pattern we are bringing in to work on in this lifetime. Then, when we grow up, we usually point our fingers accusingly at our parents and whimper, "You did it to me." But really, we chose them because they were perfect for what we wanted to work on overcoming.

We learn our belief systems as very little children, and then we move through life creating experiences to match our beliefs. Look back in your own life and notice how often you have gone through the same experience. Well, I believe you created those experiences over and over because they mirrored something you believed about yourself. It doesn't really matter how long we have had a problem, or how big it is, or how life-threatening it is.

The Point of Power is Always in the Present Moment

All the events you have experienced in your lifetime up to this moment have been created by your thoughts and beliefs you have held in the past. They were created by the thoughts and words you used yesterday, last week, last month, last year, 10, 20, 30, 40 or more years ago, depending on how old you are.

However, that is your past. It is over and done with. What is important in this moment is what you are choosing to think and believe and say right now. For these thoughts and words will create your future. Your point of power is in this present moment and is forming the experiences of tomorrow, next week, next month, next year, etc.

You might notice what thought you are thinking at this moment. Is it negative or positive? Do you want this thought to be creating your future? Just notice and be aware.

The Only Thing We are Ever Dealing With is a Thought, and a Thought Can Be Changed

No matter what the problem is, our experiences are just outer effects of inner thoughts. Even self-hatred is only hating a thought you have about yourself. You have a thought that says, "I'm a bad person." This thought produces a feeling, and you buy into the feeling. However, if you don't have the thought, you won't have the feeling. And thoughts can be changed. Change the thought, and the feeling must go.

This is only to show us where we get many of our beliefs. But let us not use this information as an excuse to stay stuck in our pain. The past has no power over us. It doesn't matter how long we have had a negative pattern. The point of power is in the present moment. What a wonderful thing to realize! We can begin to be free in this moment!

Believe It or Not, We Do Choose our Thoughts

We may habitually think the same thought over and over so that it does not seem we are choosing the thought. But we did make the original choice. We can refuse to think certain thoughts. Look how often you have refused to think a positive thought about yourself. Well, you can also refuse to think a negative thought about yourself.

It seems to me that everyone on this planet who I know or have worked with is suffering from self-hatred and guilt to one degree or another. The more self-hatred and guilt we have, the less our life

works. The less self-hatred and guilt we have, the better our lives
work, on all levels.

The Innermost Belief for Everyone I Have Worked With is Always, "I'm Not Good Enough!"

We often add to that, "And I don't do enough," or "I don't
deserve." Does this sound like you? Often saying or implying or
feeling that, "You are not good enough?" But for whom? And
according to whose standards?

If this belief is very strong in you, then how can you possibly
have created a loving, joyous, prosperous, healthy life? Somehow
your main subconscious belief would always be contradicting it.
Somehow you would never quite get it together, for something
would always be going wrong somewhere.

I Find that Resentment, Criticism, Guilt, and Fear Cause More Problems Than Anything Else

These four things cause the major problems in our bodies and in
our lives. These feelings come from blaming others and not taking
responsibility for our own experiences. You see, if we are all 100%
responsible for everything in our lives, then there is no one to
blame. Whatever is happening "out there" is only a mirror of our
own inner thinking. I am not condoning other people's poor behavior, but it is *OUR* beliefs that attract people who will treat us
that way.

If you find yourself saying, "Everyone always does such and
such to me, criticizes me, is never there for me, uses me like a door
mat, abuses me," then this is *YOUR PATTERN*. There is some
thought in you that attracts people who exhibit this behavior. When
you no longer think that way, they will go elsewhere and do that to
somebody else. You will no longer attract them.

Following are some results of patterns that manifest on the
physical level: Resentment that is long held can eat away at the
body and become the disease we call cancer. Criticism as a perma-

nent habit can often lead to arthritis in the body. Guilt always looks for punishment, and punishment creates pain. (When a client comes to me with a lot of pain I know they are holding a lot of guilt). Fear, and the tension it produces, can create things like baldness, ulcers, and even sore feet.

I have found that forgiving and releasing resentment will dissolve even cancer. While this may sound simplistic, I have seen and experienced it working.

We Can Change Our Attitude Toward the Past

The past is over and done. We cannot change that now. Yet we can change our thoughts about the past. How foolish for us to *PUNISH OURSELVES* in the present moment because someone hurt us in the long ago past.

I often say to people who have deep resentment patterns, "Please begin to dissolve the resentment now, when it is relatively easy. Don't wait until you are under the threat of a surgeon's knife or on your death bed, when you may have to deal with panic, too."

When we are in a state of panic, it is very difficult to focus our minds on the healing work. We have to take time out to dissolve the fears first.

If we choose to believe we are helpless victims and that it's all hopeless, then the Universe will support us in that belief, and we will just go down the drain. It is vital that we release these foolish, outmoded, negative ideas and beliefs that do not support us and nourish us. Even our concept of God needs to be one that is *for* us, not against us.

To Release the Past, We Must Be Willing to Forgive

We need to choose to release the past and forgive everyone, ourselves included. We may not know how to forgive, and we may not want to forgive; but the very fact we say we are willing to forgive begins the healing process. It is imperative for our own healing that "we" release the past and forgive everyone.

"I forgive you for not being the way I wanted you to be. I forgive you and I set you free."

This affirmation sets *us* free.

All Disease Comes From a State of Unforgiveness

Whenever we are ill, we need to search our hearts to see who it is we need to forgive.

The *Course in Miracles* says that "All disease comes from a state of unforgiveness," and that "Whenever we are ill, we need to look around to see who it is that we need to forgive."

I would add to that concept that the very person you find it hardest to forgive is the one *YOU NEED TO LET GO OF THE MOST.* Forgiveness means giving up, letting go. It has nothing to do with condoning behavior. It's just letting the whole thing go. We do not have to know *HOW* to forgive. All we need to do is to be *WILLING* to forgive. The Universe will take care of the hows.

We understand our own pain so well. How hard it is for most of us to understand that *THEY,* whoever they are we need most to forgive, were also in pain. We need to understand that they were doing the best they could with the understanding, awareness, and knowledge they had at that time.

When people come to me with a problem, I don't care what it is — poor health, lack of money, unfulfilling relationships, or stifled creativity — there is only one thing I ever work on, and that is *LOVING THE SELF.*

I find that when we really love and accept and *APPROVE OF OURSELVES EXACTLY AS WE ARE,* then everything in life works. It's as if little miracles are everywhere. Our health improves, we attract more money, our relationships become much more fulfilling, and we begin to express ourselves in creatively fulfilling ways. All this seems to happen without our even trying.

Loving and approving of yourself, creating a space of safety, trusting and deserving and accepting, will create organization in your mind, create more loving relationships in your life, attract a new job and a new and better place to live, and even enable your body weight to normalize. People who love themselves and their bodies neither abuse themselves nor others.

Self-approval and self-acceptance in the now are the main keys to positive changes in every area of our lives.

Loving the self, to me, begins with never ever criticizing ourselves for anything. Criticism locks us into the very pattern we are trying to change. Understanding and being gentle with ourselves helps us to move out of it. Remember, you have been criticizing yourself for years, and it hasn't worked. Try approving of yourself and see what happens.

*In the infinity of life where I am,
all is perfect, whole and complete.
I believe in a power far greater than I am that flows
through me every moment of every day.
I open myself to the wisdom within,
knowing that there is only One Intelligence
in this Universe. Out of this One Intelligence
comes all the answers, all the solutions,
all the healings, all the new creations.
I trust this Power and Intelligence,
knowing that whatever I need to know is revealed to me
and that whatever I need comes to me
in the right time, space, and sequence.
All is well in my world.*

Part 2

A SESSION WITH LOUISE

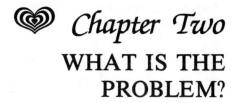 *Chapter Two*
WHAT IS THE PROBLEM?

"It is safe to look within."

My Body Doesn't Work

It hurts, bleeds, aches, oozes, twists, blows up, limps, burns, ages, can't see, can't hear, is rotting away, etc. Plus whatever else you may have created. I think I have heard them all.

My Relationships Don't Work

They are smothering, absent, demanding, don't support me, always criticizing me, unloving, never leave me alone, pick on me all the time, don't want to be bothered with me, walk all over me, never listen to me, etc. Plus whatever else you may have created. Yes, I have heard them all, too.

My Finances Don't Work

They are nonexistent, seldom there, never enough, just out of reach, go out faster than they come in, won't cover the bills, slip through my fingers, etc. Plus whatever else you may have created. Of course, I have heard them all.

My Life Doesn't Work

I never get to do what I want to do. I can't please anyone. I don't know what I want to do. There is never any time for me. My needs and desires are always left out. I'm only doing this to please them. I am just a doormat. Nobody cares what I want to do. I have no talent. I can't do anything right. All I do is procrastinate. Nothing ever works for me, etc. Plus whatever else you have created for yourself. All these I have heard and more.

Whenever I ask a new client what is going on in his or her life, I usually get one of the above answers. Or maybe several of these answers. They really think they know the problem. But I know these complaints are only outer effects of inner thought patterns. Beneath the inner thought patterns is another deeper, more fundamental pattern that is the basis of all the outer effects.

I listen to the words they use as I ask some basic questions:

> What is happening in your life?
> How is your health?
> What do you do for a living?
> Do you like your work?
> How are your finances?
> How is your love life?
> How did the last relationship end?
> And the relationship before that, how did it end?
> Tell me about your childhood, briefly.

I watch the body postures and the facial movements. But mostly I really listen to the words they say. Thoughts and words create our future experiences. As I listen to them talk, I can readily understand why they have these particular problems. The words we speak are indicative of our inner thoughts. Sometimes the words they use do not match the experiences they describe. Then I know either they are not in touch with what is really going on or they are lying to me. Either one is a starting point and gives us a basis from which to begin.

Exercise: I Should

The next thing I do is to give them a pad and pen and ask them to write on the top of the page:

I SHOULD

_____ .
_____ .
_____ .
_____ .
_____ .

They are to make a list of five or six ways to finish that sentence. Some people find it difficult to begin, and some have so many things to write it's hard for them to stop.

I then ask them to read the list to me one at a time beginning each sentence with "I Should . . ." As they read each one I ask, "Why?"

The answers that come out are interesting and revealing, such as:

> My mother said I should.
> Because I am afraid not to.
> Because I have to be perfect.
> Well, everybody has to do that.
> Because I am too lazy, too short, too tall, too fat, too thin, too dumb, too ugly, too worthless.

These answers show me where they are stuck in their beliefs and what they think their limitations are.

I make no comments on their answers. When they are through with their list, I talk about the word *SHOULD*.

You see, I believe that should is one of the most damaging words in our language. Every time we use should we are in effect saying "wrong." Either we *are* wrong or we *were* wrong or we are *going to be* wrong. I don't think we need more wrongs in our life. We need to have more freedom of choice. I would like to take the word *SHOULD* and remove it from the vocabulary forever. I replace it with the word *COULD.* Could gives us choice and we are never wrong.

I then ask them to reread the list one item at a time, except this time to begin each sentence by saying, "If I really wanted to, I could _____." This puts a whole new light on the subject.

As they do this, I ask them gently, "Why haven't you?" Now we hear different answers:

I don't want to.
I am afraid.
I don't know how.
Because I am not good enough.
Etc.

We often find they have been berating themselves for years for something they never wanted to do in the first place. Or they have been criticizing themselves for not doing something when it was never their idea to begin with. Often it was just something that someone else said they should do. When they can see that, they can just drop it from the "should list." What a relief that is.

Look at all the people who try to force themselves for years into a career they don't even like only because their parents said they should become a dentist or a teacher. How often have we felt inferior because we were told we should be smarter or richer or more creative like some relative.

What is there on your "should list" that could be dropped with a sense of relief?

By the time we have gone through this short list, they are beginning to look at their life in a new and different way. They notice that many of the things they thought they should do are things they never wanted to do and that they were only trying to please other people. So many times it is because they are afraid or feel they are not good enough.

The problem has now begun to shift. I have started the process of releasing the feeling of "being wrong" because they are not fitting someone else's standards.

Next I begin to explain to them *my philosophy of life* as I did in Chapter One. I believe life is really very simple. What we give out, we get back. The Universe totally supports every thought we choose to think and to believe. When we are little we learn how to feel about ourselves and about life by the reactions of the adults around us. Whatever these beliefs are, they will be recreated as experiences as we grow up. However, we are only dealing with thought patterns, and *the point of power is always in the present moment.* Changes can begin in this moment.

Loving the Self

I continue to explain that no matter what their problem seems to be, there is only one thing I ever work on with anyone, and this is *Loving the Self.* Love is the miracle cure. Loving ourselves works miracles in our lives.

I am not talking about vanity or arrogance or being stuck-up, for that is not love. It is only fear. I am talking about having a great respect for ourselves and a gratitude for the miracle of our body and our mind.

"Love" to me is appreciation to such a degree that it fills my heart to bursting and overflows. Love can go in any direction. I can feel love for:

> The very process of life itself.
> The joy of being alive.
> The beauty I see.
> Another person.
> Knowledge.
> The process of the mind.
> Our bodies and the way they work.
> Animals, birds, fishes.
> Vegetation in all its forms.
> The Universe and the way it works.

What can you add to this list?

Let's look at some of the ways we don't love ourselves:
We scold and criticize ourselves endlessly.
We mistreat our bodies with food, alcohol, and drugs.
We choose to believe we are unlovable.
We are afraid to charge a decent price for our services.
We create illnesses and pain in our bodies.
We procrastinate on things that would benefit us.
We live in chaos and disorder.
We create debt and burdens.
We attract lovers and mates that belittle us.

What are some of your ways?

If we *deny our good* in any way, it is an act of not loving ourselves. I remember a client I worked with who wore glasses. One day we released an old fear from childhood. The next day she awakened to find her contact lenses were bothering her too much to wear. She looked around and found her eyesight was perfectly clear.

Yet she spent the whole day saying, "I don't believe it, I don't believe it." The next day she was back to wearing contacts. Our subconscious mind has no sense of humor. She couldn't believe she had created perfect eyesight.

Lack of self-worth is another expression of not loving ourselves.

Tom was a very good artist, and he had some wealthy clients who asked him to decorate a wall or two in their homes. Yet somehow he was always behind in his own bill paying. His original quote was never enough to cover the time involved to complete the work. Anyone who gives a service or creates a one-of-a-kind product can charge any price. People with wealth love to pay a lot for what they get; it gives the item more value. More examples:

Our partner is tired and grouchy. We wonder what *we* have done wrong to cause it.

He takes us out once or twice and never calls again. We think something must be wrong with *us*.

Our marriage ends and we are sure *we* are a failure.

We are afraid to ask for a raise.

Our bodies do not match those in *Gentleman's Quarterly* or *Vogue* magazine, and we feel inferior.

We don't "make the sale," or "get the part," and we are sure we are "not good enough."

We are afraid of intimacy and allowing anyone to get too close, so we have anonymous sex.

We can't make decisions because we are sure they will be wrong.

How do you express *your* lack of self-worth?

The Perfection of Babies

How perfect you were when you were a tiny baby. Babies do not have to do anything to become perfect, they already are perfect, and they act as if they know it. They know they are the center of the Universe. They are not afraid to ask for what they want. They freely express their emotions. You know when a baby is angry, in fact, the whole neighborhood knows. You also know when they are happy, for their smiles light up a room. They are full of love.

Tiny babies will die if they do not get love. Once we are older, we learn to live without love, but babies will not stand for it. Babies also love every part of their bodies, even their own feces. They have incredible courage.

You were like that. We were all like that. Then we began to listen to adults around us who had learned to be fearful, and we began to deny our own magnificence.

I never believe it when clients try to convince me how terrible they are, or how unlovable they are. My work is to bring them back to the time when they knew how to really love themselves.

Exercise: Mirror

Next I ask the client to pick up a small mirror, look into their eyes and say their name and, "I love and accept you exactly as you are."

This is *so* difficult for many people. Seldom do I get a calm reaction, let alone enjoyment from this exercise. Some cry or are close to tears, some get angry, some belittle their features or qualities, some insist they *CAN'T* do it. I even had one man throw the mirror across the room and want to run away. It took him several months before he could begin to relate to himself in the mirror.

For years I looked into the mirror only to criticize what I saw there. Recalling the endless hours I spent plucking my eyebrows trying to make myself barely acceptable amuses me now. I remember it used to frighten me to look into my own eyes.

This simple exercise shows me so much. In less than an hour I am able to get to some of the core issues that are beneath the outer problem. If we work only on the level of the problem, we can spend endless time working out each and every detail; and the minute we think we have it all "fixed up," it will crop up somewhere else.

"The Problem" is Rarely the Real Problem

She was so concerned with her looks, and especially with her teeth. She went from dentist to dentist feeling each one had only made her look worse. She went to have her nose fixed and they did a poor job. Each professional was mirroring her belief that she was ugly. Her problem was not her looks, but that she was convinced something was wrong with her.

There was another woman who had terrible breath. It was uncomfortable to be around her. She was studying to be a minister, and her outer demeanor was pious and spiritual. Beneath this was a raging current of anger and jealousy that exploded now and then when she thought someone might be threatening her position. Her inner thoughts were expressed through her breath, and she was offensive even when she pretended to be loving. No one threatened her but herself.

He was only fifteen when his mother brought him to me with Hodgkin's disease and three months to live. His mother was understandably hysterical and difficult to deal with, but the boy was bright and clever and wanted to live. He was willing to do anything I told him to, including changing the way he thought and spoke. His separated parents were always arguing, and he really did not have a settled home life.

He wanted desperately to be an actor. The pursuit of fame and fortune far outweighed his ability to experience joy. He thought he could be acceptable and worthwhile only if he had fame. I taught him to love and accept himself, and he got well. He is now grown up and appears on Broadway with regularity. As he learned to experience the joy of being himself, the parts in plays opened up for him.

Overweight is another good example of how we can waste a lot of energy trying to correct a problem that is not the real problem. People often spend years and years fighting fat and are still overweight. They blame all their problems on being overweight. The excess weight is only an outer effect of a deep inner problem. To me, it is always fear and a need for protection. When we feel frightened or insecure or "not good enough," many of us will put on extra weight for protection.

To spend our time berating ourselves for being too heavy, to feel guilty about every bite of food we eat, to do all the numbers we do on ourselves when we gain weight, are just a waste of time. Twenty years later we can still be in the same situation because we have not even begun to deal with the real problem. All we have done is to make ourselves more frightened and insecure, and then we need more weight for protection.

So I refuse to focus on excess weight or on diets. For diets do not work. The only diet that does work is a mental diet; dieting from negative thoughts. I say to clients, "Let us just put that issue to one side for the time being while we work on a few other things first."

They will often tell me they can't love themselves because they are so fat, or as one girl put it, "too round at the edges." I explain that they are fat because they don't love themselves. When we begin to love and approve of ourselves, it's amazing how weight just disappears from our bodies.

Sometimes clients even get angry with me as I explain how simple it is to change their lives. They may feel I do not understand their problems. One woman became very upset and said, "I came here to get help with my dissertation, not to learn to love myself." To me it was so obvious that her main problem was a lot of self-hatred, and this permeated every part of her life, including writing her dissertation. She could not succeed at anything as long as she felt so worthless.

She couldn't hear me and left in tears, coming back one year later with the same problem plus a lot of other problems. Some people are not ready; and there is not judgment. We all begin to make our changes in the right time, space, sequence for *us*. I did not even begin to make my changes until I was in my forties.

The Real Problem

So here is a client who has just looked into the harmless little mirror, and he or she is all upset. I smile with delight and say, "Good, now we are looking at the 'real problem,' now we can begin to clear out what is really standing in your way." I talk more about loving the self, about how, for me, loving the self begins with never, ever criticizing ourselves for anything.

I watch their faces as I ask them if they criticize themselves. Their reactions tell me so much:

Well, of course I do.
All the time.
Not as much as I used to.
Well, how am I going to change if I don't criticize myself?
Doesn't everyone?

To the latter I answer, "We are not talking about everyone, we are talking about you. Why do you criticize yourself? What is wrong with you?"

As they talk I make a list. What they say often coincides with their "should list." They feel they are too tall, too short, too fat, too thin, too dumb, too old, too young, too ugly. (The most beautiful or handsome will often say this.) Or they're too late, too early, too lazy, and on and on. Notice how it is almost always "too" something. Finally we get down to the bottom line and they say, "I am not good enough."

Hurrah, hurrah! We have finally found the central issue. They criticize themselves because they have learned to believe they "are not good enough." Clients are always amazed at how fast we have gotten to this point. Now we do not have to bother with any of the side effects like body problems, relationship problems, money problems, or lack of creative expressions. We can put all our energy into dissolving the cause of the whole thing: *"NOT LOVING THE SELF!"*

In the infinity of life where I am,
all is perfect, whole and complete.
I am always Divinely protected and guided.
It is safe for me to look within myself.
It is safe for me to look into the past.
It is safe for me to enlarge my viewpoint of life.
I am far more than my personality – past, present or future.
I now choose to rise above my personality problems
to recognize the magnificence of my being.
I am totally willing to learn to love myself.
All is well in my world.

♥ Chapter Three
WHERE DOES IT COME FROM?

"The past has no power over me."

All right, we have gone through a lot of stuff, and we have sifted through what we *thought* the problem was. Now we have come up with what I believe is the real problem. We feel we are *not good enough*, and there is a *lack of self-love*. From the way I look at life, if there is any problem, then this has to be true. So let us look at where this belief came from.

How did we go from being a tiny baby who knows the perfection of itself and of life to being a person who has problems and feels unworthy and unlovable to one degree or another? People who already love themselves can love themselves even more.

Think of a rose from the time it is a tiny bud. As it opens to full flower, till the last petal falls, it is always beautiful, always perfect, always changing. So it is with us. We are always perfect, always beautiful, and ever changing. We are doing the best we can with the understanding, awareness and knowledge we have. As we gain more understanding, awareness and knowledge, we will do things differently.

Mental Housecleaning

Now is the time to examine our past a bit more, to take a look at some of the beliefs that have been running us.

Some people find this part of the cleansing process very painful, but it need not be. We must look at what is there before we can clean it out.

If you want to clean a room thoroughly, you will pick up and examine everything in it. Some things you will look at with love and you will dust them or polish them to give them new beauty. Some things you will see that need refinishing or repair, and you will make a note to do that. Some things will never serve you again, and it becomes time to let those things go. Old magazines and newspapers and dirty paper plates can be dropped into the waste basket very calmly. There is no need to get angry in order to clean a room.

It is the same thing when we are cleaning our mental house. There is no need to get angry just because some of the beliefs in it are ready to be tossed out. Let them go as easily as you would scrape bits of food into the trash after a meal. Would you really dig into yesterday's garbage to make tonight's meal? Do you dig into old *mental* garbage to create tomorrow's experiences?

If a thought or belief does not serve you, let it go! There is no written law that says that because you once believed something you have to continue to believe it forever.

So let's look at some of these limiting beliefs and where they came from:

LIMITING BELIEF: "I'm not good enough."
WHERE IT CAME FROM: A father who repeatedly told him he was stupid.

He said he wanted to be a success so his daddy would be proud of him. But he was riddled with guilt, which created resentment, and all he could produce was one failure after another. Daddy kept financing businesses for him, and one after another, they failed. He used failure to get even. He made his daddy pay and pay and pay. Of course, *he* was the biggest loser.

LIMITING BELIEF: Lack of self-love.
WHERE IT CAME FROM: Trying to win daddy's approval.

The last thing she wanted was to be like her father. They couldn't agree on anything and were always arguing. She only wanted his approval, but instead all she got was criticism. Her body was full of pains. Her father had exactly the same kind of pains. She did not realize her anger was creating her pains just as her father's anger was creating pain for him.

LIMITING BELIEF: Life is dangerous.
WHERE IT CAME FROM: A frightened father.
Another client saw life as grim and harsh. It was difficult for her to laugh; and when she did, she would become frightened that something "bad" would happen. She had been reared with the admonition, "Don't laugh or *'they'* might get you."

LIMITING BELIEF: I'm not good enough.
WHERE IT CAME FROM: Being abandoned and ignored.
It was difficult for him to talk. Silence had become a way of life for him. He had just come off drugs and alcohol and was convinced that he was terrible. I discovered his mother had died when he was very young, and he had been reared by an aunt. The aunt seldom spoke except to give an order, and he was brought up in silence. He even ate alone in silence and stayed quietly in his room day after day. He had a lover who was also a silent man, and they spent most of their time alone in silence. The lover died, and once again he was alone.

Exercise: Negative Messages

The next exercise we do is to get a large sheet of paper and make a list of all the things your parents said were wrong with you. What were the negative messages you heard? Give yourself enough time to remember as many as you can. A half hour usually works well.

What did they say about money? What did they say about your body? What did they say about love and relationships? What did they say about your creative talents? What were the limiting or negative things they said to you?

If you can, just look objectively at these items and say to

yourself, *"So that's where that belief came from."*

Now let's take a new sheet of paper and dig a little deeper. What other negative messages did you hear as a child?

From relatives _____

From teachers _____

From friends _____

From authority figures _____

From your church _____

Write them all down. Take your time. Be aware of what feelings are going on in your body.

What you have on these two pieces of paper are the thoughts that need to be removed from your consciousness. These are the very beliefs you have that are making you feel "not good enough."

Seeing Yourself as a Child

If we were to take a three-year-old child and put him in the middle of the room, and you and I were to start yelling at the child, telling him how stupid he was, how he could never do anything right, how he should do this, and shouldn't do that, and look at the mess he made; and maybe hit him a few times, we would end up with a frightened little child who sits docily in the corner; or who tears up the place. The child will go one of these two ways, but we will never know the potential of that child.

If we take the same little child and tell him how much we love him, how much we care, that we love the way he looks and love how bright and clever he is, that we love the way he does things and that it's okay for him to make mistakes as he learns — and that we will always be there for him no matter what — then the potential that comes out of that child will blow your mind!

Each one of us has a three-year-old child within us, and we often spend most of our time yelling at that kid in ourselves. Then we wonder why our lives don't work.

If you had a friend who was always criticizing you, would you want to be around that person? Perhaps you were treated this way as a child, and that is sad. However, that was a long time ago, and if you are now choosing to treat yourself in the same way, then it is sadder still.

So now, here in front of us, we have a list of the negative messages we heard as a child. How does this list correspond with what *you* believe to be wrong with you? Are they almost the same? Probably yes.

We base our life script on our early messages. We are all good little children and obediently accept what "they" tell us as truth. It would be very easy just to blame our parents and be victims for the rest of our lives. But that wouldn't be very much fun, and it certainly wouldn't get us out of our stuck position.

Blaming Your Family

Blame is one of the surest ways to stay *in* a problem. In blaming another, we give away our power. Understanding enables us to rise above the issue and take control of our future.

The past cannot be changed. The future is shaped by our current thinking. It is imperative for our freedom to understand that our parents were doing the best they could with the understanding, awareness, and knowledge they had. Whenever we blame someone else, we are not taking responsibility for ourselves.

Those people who did all those terrible things to us were just as frightened and scared as you are. They felt just the same helplessness as you do. The only things they could possibly teach you are what they had been taught.

How much do you know about your parents' childhoods, especially before the age of ten? If it's still possible for you to find out, ask them. If you're able to find out about your parents' childhoods, you will more easily understand why they did what they did. Understanding will bring you compassion.

If you don't know and can't find out, try to imagine what it must have been like for them. What kind of childhood would create an adult like that?

You need this knowledge for your own freedom. You can't free yourself until you free them. You can't forgive yourself until you forgive them. If you demand perfection from them, you will demand perfection from yourself, and you will be miserable all your life.

Choosing Our Parents

I agree with the theory that we choose our parents. The lessons we learn seem perfectly matched to the "weaknesses" of the parents we have.

I believe we are all on an endless journey through eternity. We come to this planet to learn particular lessons that are necessary for our spiritual evolution. We choose our sex, our color, our country; and then we look around for the perfect set of parents who will "mirror" our patterns.

Our visits to this planet are like going to school. If you want to become a beautician, you go to beauty school. If you want to become a mechanic, you go to mechanics school. If you want to become a lawyer, you go to law school. The parents you picked this time around are the perfect couple who are "experts" in what you have chosen to learn.

When we grow up, we have a tendency to point our fingers accusingly at our parents and say, "You did it to me!" But I believe we chose them.

Listening to Others

Our older brothers and sisters are gods to us when we are little. If they were unhappy, they probably took it out on us physically or verbally. They might have said things like:

"I'll tell on you for . . ." (instilling guilt)

"You're just a baby, you can't do that."

"You're too stupid to play with us."

Teachers at school often influence us greatly. In the fifth grade, a teacher told me emphatically I was too tall to be a dancer. I believed her and put away my dancing ambitions until I was too old to make dancing a career.

Did you understand that tests and grades were only to see how much knowledge you had at a given time, or were you a child who allowed tests and grades to measure self-worth?

Our early friends share their own misinformation about life with us. The other kids at school can tease us and leave lasting hurts. When I was a child, my last name was Lunney and the kids used to call me "lunatic."

Neighbors also have an influence, not only because of their remarks but also because we're asked, "What will the neighbors think?"

Think back to what other authority figures were influential in your childhood.

And, of course, there are the strong and very persuasive statements made by advertisements in periodicals and on television. All too many products are sold by making us feel we are unworthy or wrong if we don't use them.

*   *   *

We are all here to transcend our early limitations, whatever they were. We're here to recognize our own magnificence and divinity no matter what *they* told us. You have *your* negative beliefs to overcome, and I have *my* negative beliefs to overcome.

*In the infinity of life where I am,
all is perfect, whole and complete.
The past has no power over me
because I am willing to learn and to change.
I see the past as necessary to bring me to where I am today.
I am willing to begin where I am right now
to clean the rooms of my mental house.
I know it does not matter where I start, so I now begin
with the smallest and the easiest rooms, and in that way
I will see results quickly.
I am thrilled to be in the middle of this adventure,
for I know I will never go through
this particular experience again. I am willing to set myself free.
All is well in my world.*

❤️ Chapter Four
IS IT TRUE?

"Truth is the unchangeable part of me."

The question, "Is it true or real?" has two answers: "Yes" and "No." It is true if you *believe* it to be true. It is not true if you *believe* it isn't true. The glass is both half full and half empty, depending on how you look at it. There are literally billions of thoughts we can choose to think.

Most of us choose to think the same kinds of thoughts our parents used to think, but we don't have to continue to do this. There is no law written that says we can only think in one way.

Whatever I choose to believe becomes true for me. Whatever you choose to believe becomes true for you. Our thoughts can be totally different. Our lives and experiences are totally different.

Examine Your Thoughts

Whatever we believe becomes true for us. If you have a sudden financial disaster, then on some level you may believe you are unworthy of being comfortable with money, or you believe in burdens and debt. Or if you believe that nothing good ever lasts, do you believe that life is out to get you, or, as I hear so often, "I just can't win."

If you seem unable to attract a relationship, you may believe "Nobody loves me," or "I am unlovable." Perhaps you fear being dominated as your mother was, or maybe you think, "People just hurt me."

If you have poor health, you may believe, "Illness runs in our family." Or that you are a victim of the weather. Or perhaps it's, "I was born to suffer," or "It's just one thing after another."

Or you may have a different belief. Perhaps you're not even aware of your belief. Most people really aren't. They just see the outer circumstances as being the way the cookie crumbles. Until someone can show you the connection between the outer experiences and the inner thoughts, you remain a victim in life.

PROBLEM	BELIEF
Financial disaster	I am not worthy of having money.
No friends	Nobody loves me.
Problems with work	I'm not good enough.
Always pleasing others	I never get my way.

Whatever the problem is, it comes from a thought pattern, and *thought patterns can be changed!*

It may feel true, it may *seem* true; all these problems we're wrestling with and juggling in our lives. However, no matter how difficult an issue we are dealing with, it is only an outer result or the effect of an inner thought pattern.

If you don't know what thoughts are creating your problems, you're in the right place now, because this book is designed to help you find out. Look at the problems in your life. *Ask yourself, "What kinds of thoughts am I having that create this?"*

If you allow yourself to sit quietly and ask this question, your inner intelligence will show you the answer.

It's Only a Belief You Learned as a Child

Some of the things we believe *are* positive and nourishing. These thoughts serve us well all of our lives, such as, "Look both ways before you cross the street."

Other thoughts are very useful at the beginning, but as we grow older they are no longer appropriate. "Don't trust strangers" may be good advice for a small child; but for an adult, to continue this belief will only create isolation and loneliness.

Why do we so seldom sit down and ask ourselves, "Is that really true?" For instance, why do I believe things like, "It's difficult for me to learn." "Is it true for me now?" "Where did that belief come from?" "Do I still believe it because a first grade teacher told me that over and over?" "Would I be better off if I dropped that belief?"

Beliefs that "Boys don't cry," and "Girls don't climb trees," create men who hide their feelings and women who are afraid to be physical.

If we were taught as a child that the world is a frightening place, then everything we hear that fits that belief we will accept as true for us. The same is true for "Don't trust strangers," "Don't go out at night," or "People cheat you."

On the other hand, if we were taught early in life that the world is a safe place, then we would hold other beliefs. We could easily accept that love is everywhere and people are so friendly and I always have whatever I need.

If you were taught as a child that, "It's all my fault," then you will walk around always feeling guilt no matter what happens. Your belief will turn you into someone who's always saying, "I'm sorry."

If you learned to believe as a child, "I don't count," then this belief will always keep you at the end of the line wherever you are. Like my childhood experience about not getting any cake. Sometimes you will feel you're invisible when others fail to notice you.

Did your childhood circumstances teach you to believe, "Nobody loves me"? Then you are sure to be lonely. Even when you bring a friend or relationship into your life, it will be short-lived.

Did your family teach you, "There is not enough." Then I am sure you often feel as though the cupboard is bare or you find you just get by or are always in debt.

I had a client who had been brought up in a household where they believed everything was wrong and could only get worse. His main joy in life was playing tennis, and then he hurt his knee. He went to every doctor he could find, and it only got worse. Finally he could not play at all.

Another person had been brought up as a preacher's son, and as a child he was taught that everybody else comes first. The preacher's family always came last. Today he is wonderful at helping his clients get the best deal, yet he's usually in debt with little pocket money. His belief still makes him last in line.

If You Believe It, It Seems True

How often have we said, "That's the way I am," or "That's the way it is." Those specific words are really saying that that's what we *believe* to be true for us. Usually, what we believe is only someone else's opinion we have incorporated into our belief systems. No doubt it fits right in with all the other things we believe.

Are you one of the many people who will get up in the morning, see that it's raining, and say, "Oh, what a lousy day!"

It is *not* a lousy day. It is only a wet day. If we wear the appropriate clothing and change our attitude, we can have a lot of rainy day fun. If it is really our belief that rainy days are lousy days, then we will always greet rain with a sinking heart. We will fight the day rather than flow with what is happening in the moment.

There is no "good" or "bad" weather, there is just weather and our individual reactions to it.

If we want a joyous life, we must think joyous thoughts. If we want a prosperous life, we must think prosperous thoughts. If we want a loving life, we must think loving thoughts. *Whatever we send out mentally or verbally will come back to us in like form.*

Each Moment is a New Beginning

I repeat, *The Point of Power is always in the present moment.* You are *never* stuck. This is where the changes take place, right here and right now *in our own minds!* It doesn't matter how long we've had a negative pattern or an illness or a poor relationship or lack of finances or self-hatred. We can begin to make a shift today!

Your problem no longer needs to be the truth for you. It can now fade back to the nothingness from whence it came. You can do it.

Remember: *you are the only person who thinks in your mind!* You are the power and authority in your world!

Your thoughts and beliefs of the past have created this moment, and all the moments up to this moment. What you are now choosing to believe and think and say will create the next moment and the next day and the next month and the next year.

Yes, you darling! I can give you the most marvelous advice, coming from my years of experience, yet you can continue to choose to think the same old thoughts, you can refuse to change and keep all your problems.

You are the power in your world! You get to have whatever you choose to think!

This moment begins the new process. Each moment is a new beginning, and this moment is a new beginning for you right here and right now! Isn't that great to know! This moment is the *Point of Power!* This moment is where the change begins!

Is It True?

Stop for a moment and catch your thought. What are you thinking right now? If it is true that your thoughts shape your life, would you want what you were just thinking right now to become true for you? If it's a thought of worry or anger or hurt or revenge or fear, how do you think this thought will come back to you?

It is not always easy to catch our thoughts because they move so swiftly. However, we can begin right now to watch and listen to what we say. If you hear yourself expressing negative words of any sort, stop in midsentence. Either rephrase the sentence or just drop it. You could even say to it, "Out!"

Imagine yourself in line at a cateteria, or perhaps at a buffet in a

luxurious hotel, where instead of dishes of food there are dishes of
thoughts. You get to choose any and all thoughts you wish. These
thoughts will create your future experiences.

Now if you choose thoughts that will create problems and pain,
that's rather foolish. It's like choosing food that always makes you
ill. We may do this once or twice; but as soon as we learn which
foods upset our bodies, we stay away from them. It's the same
with thoughts. *Let us stay away from thoughts that create problems and pain.*

One of my early teachers, Dr. Raymond Charles Barker, would
repeatedly say, "When there is a problem, there is not something
to do, there is something to know."

Our minds create our future. When we have something in our
present that is undesirable, then we must use our minds to change
the situation. And we can begin to change it this very second.

It is my deep desire that the topic "How Your Thoughts Work,"
be the very first subject taught in school. I have never understood
the importance of having children memorize battle dates. It seems
such a waste of mental energy. Instead, we could teach them important subjects such as How the Mind Works, How to Handle
Finances, How to Invest Money for Financial Security, How to
Be a Parent, How to Create Good Relationships, and How to
Create and Maintain Self-Esteem and Self-Worth.

Can you imagine what a whole generation of adults would be
like if they had been taught these subjects in school along with
their regular curriculum? Think how these truths would manifest.
We would have happy people who feel good about themselves. We
would have people who are comfortable financially and who enrich
the economy by investing their money wisely. They would have
good relationships with everyone and would be comfortable with
the role of parenthood and then go on to create another generation
of children who feel good about themselves. Yet within all this,
each person would remain an individual expressing his or her own
creativity.

There is no time to waste. Let's continue with our work.

In the infinity of life where I am,
all is perfect, whole and complete.
I no longer choose to believe in old limitations and lacks.
I now choose to begin to see myself as the Universe sees me,
perfect, whole and complete.
The truth of my Being is that I was created
perfect, whole and complete.
I am now perfect, whole and complete.
I will always be perfect, whole and complete.
I now choose to live my life from this understanding.
I am in the right place at the right time, doing the right thing.
All is well in my world.

♡♡ *Chapter Five*
WHAT DO WE DO NOW?

"I see my patterns, and I choose to make changes."

Decide to Change

Throwing up our hands in horror at what we may call the mess of our lives and just giving up are the ways many people react at this point. Others get angry at themselves or at life and also give up.

By giving up, I mean deciding, "It's all hopeless and impossible to make any changes, so why try." The rest of it goes, "Just stay the way you are. At least you know how to handle that pain. You don't like it, but it is familiar and you hope it won't get any worse."

To me, habitual anger is like sitting in a corner with a dunce hat on. Does this sound familiar? Something happens and you get angry. Something else happens and you get angry again. Something else happens and you get angry again. Something else happens, and once again you get angry. But you never go beyond getting angry.

What good does that do? It's a foolish reaction to waste your time only getting angry. It's also a refusal to see life in a new and different way.

It would be much more helpful to ask yourself how you are creating so many situations to get angry at.

What are you believing that causes all these frustrations? What are you giving out that attracts in others the need to irritate you? Why do you believe that to get your way you need to get angry?

Whatever you give out comes back to you. The more you give out anger, the more you are creating situations for you to get angry at, like sitting in a corner with a dunce hat on getting nowhere.

Does this paragraph bring up feelings of anger? Good! It must be hitting home. This is something you could be willing to change.

Make a Decision to be "Willing to Change!"

If you really want to know how stubborn you are, just approach the idea of being *willing to change.* We all want to have our lives change, to have situations become better and easier, but *we* don't want to have to change. We would rather *they* change. In order to have this happen, *we must change inside.* We must change our way of thinking, change our way of speaking, change our way of expressing ourselves. Only then will the outer changes occur.

This is the next step. We are now fairly clear on what the problems are, and where they came from. Now it is time to be *willing to change.*

I have always had a streak of stubbornness within me. Even now sometimes when I decide to make a change in my life, this stubbornness can come to the surface and my resistance to changing *my* thinking is strong. I can temporarily become self-righteous, angry, and withdrawn.

Yes, this still goes on within me after all these years of work. It's one of my lessons. However, now when this happens, I know I'm hitting an important point of change. Every time I decide to make a change in my life, to release something else, I'm going ever deeper into myself to do this.

Each old layer must give way in order to be replaced with new thinking. Some of it is easy, and some of it is like trying to lift a boulder with a feather.

The more tenaciously I hold onto an old belief when I say I want to make a change, the more I know this is an important one for me to release. It is only by learning these things that I can teach others.

It is my opinion that many really good teachers do not come from joyful households where all was easy. They come from a place of much pain and suffering, and they've worked through the layers to reach the place where they can now help others to become free. Most good teachers are continually working to release even more, to remove ever-deeper layers of limitation. This becomes a lifetime occupation.

The main difference between the way I used to work at releasing beliefs, and the way I do it today, is that now I don't have to be angry at myself in order to do so. I no longer choose to believe that I'm a bad person just because I find something else to change within me.

Housecleaning

The mental work I do now is like cleaning a house. I go through my mental rooms and examine the thoughts and beliefs in them. Some I love, so I polish and shine them and make them even more useful. Some I notice need replacement or repair and I get around to them as I can. Some are like yesterday's newspapers and old magazines or clothing that's no longer suitable. These I either give away or toss into the trash, and I let them be gone forever.

It's not necessary for me to be angry or to feel I'm a bad person in order to do this.

Exercise: I am Willing to Change

Let's use the affirmation, "I am willing to change." Repeat this often. "I am willing to change. I am willing to change." You can touch your throat as you say this. The throat is the energy center in the body where change takes place. By touching your throat, you are acknowledging you are in the process of changing.

Be willing to allow the changes to happen when they come up in your life. Be aware that where you *DO NOT*

WANT TO CHANGE is exactly the area where you *NEED* to change the most. "I am willing to change."

The Universal Intelligence is always responding to your thoughts and words. Things will definitely begin to change as you make these statements.

Many Ways to Change

Working with my ideas is not the only way to change. There are many other methods that work quite well. In the back of the book, I have included a list of many of the ways you could approach your own growth process.

Just think of a few now. There is the spiritual approach, there is the mental approach, and the physical approach. Holistic healing includes body, mind, and spirit. You can begin in any one of these areas as long as you eventually include all the areas. Some begin with the mental approach and do workshops or therapy. Some begin in the spiritual area with meditation or prayer.

When you begin to *clean your house,* it really doesn't matter which room you start in. Just begin in the area that appeals to you most. The others will happen almost by themselves.

Junk food eaters who begin on the spiritual level often find that they are drawn to nutrition. They meet a friend or find a book or go to a class that brings them to an understanding that what they put into their bodies will have a lot to do with how they feel and look. One level will always lead to another as long as there is the willingness to grow and change.

I give very little nutritional advice because I have discovered that all systems work for some people. I do have a local network of good practitioners in the holistic field, and I refer clients to them when I see the necessity for nutritional knowledge. This is an area where you must find your own way or go to a specialist who can test you.

Many of the books on nutrition have been written by persons who were very ill and worked out a system for their own healing. Then they wrote a book to tell everyone else the methods they used. However, everyone is not alike.

For instance, the macrobiotic and the natural raw food diets are two totally different approaches. The raw food people never cook anything, seldom eat bread or grains, and are very careful not to eat fruits and vegetables at the same meal. And they never use salt. The macrobiotic people cook almost all of their food, have a different system of food combining, and use a lot of salt. Both systems work. Both systems have healed bodies. But neither system is good for everybody's body.

My personal nutritional approach is simple. If it grows, eat it. If it doesn't grow, don't eat it.

Be conscious of your eating. It's like paying attention to our thoughts. We also can learn to pay attention to our bodies and the signals we get when we eat in different ways.

Cleaning the mental house after a lifetime of indulging in negative mental thoughts is a bit like going on a good nutritional program after a lifetime of indulging in junk foods. They both can often create healing crises. As you begin to change your physical diet, the body begins to throw off the accumulation of toxic residue, and as this happens you can feel rather rotten for a day or two. So it is when you make a decision to change the mental thought patterns, your circumstances can begin to seem worse for a while.

Recall for a moment the end of a Thanksgiving dinner. The food is eaten and it's time to clean the turkey pan. The pan is all burnt and crusty, so you put in hot water and soap and let it soak for a while. Then you begin to scrape the pan. Now you *really* have a mess; it looks worse than ever. But, if you just keep scrubbing away, soon you will have a pan as good as new.

It's the same thing with cleaning up a dried-on crusty mental pattern. When we soak it with new ideas all the gook comes to the surface to look at. Just keep doing the new affirmations, and soon you will have totally cleared an old limitation.

Exercise: Willing to Change

So we have decided we are willing to change, and we will use any and all methods that work for us. Let me describe one of the methods I use with myself and with others.

First: go look in a mirror and say to yourself, "I am willing to change."

Notice how you feel. If you are hesitant or resistant or just don't want to change, ask yourself why. What old belief are you holding on to? Please don't scold yourself, just notice what it is. I'll bet that belief has been causing you a lot of trouble. I wonder where it came from. Do you know?

Whether we know where it came from or not, let's do something to dissolve it, now. Again go to the mirror and looking deep into your own eyes, touch your throat and say out loud ten times, "I am willing to release all resistance."

Mirror work is very powerful. As children we received most of our negative messages from others looking us straight in the eye and perhaps shaking a finger at us. Whenever we look into the mirror today, most of us will say something negative to ourselves. We either criticize our looks or berate ourselves for something. To look yourself straight in the eye and make a positive declaration about yourself is, in my opinion, the quickest way to get results with affirmations.

In the infinity of life where I am,
all is perfect, whole and complete.
I now choose calmly and objectively to see my old patterns
and I am willing to make changes.
I am teachable. I can learn. I am willing to change.
I choose to have fun doing this.
I choose to react as though I have found a treasure
when I discover something else to release.
I see and feel myself changing moment by moment.
Thoughts no longer have any power over me.
I am the power in my world. I choose to be free.
All is well in my world.

♥ Chapter Six
RESISTANCE TO CHANGE

"I am in the rhythm and flow of ever-changing life."

Awareness is the First Step in Healing or Changing

When we have some pattern buried deeply within us, we must become aware of it in order to heal the condition. Perhaps we begin to mention the condition, to complain about it or to see it in other people. It rises to the surface of our attention in some way, and we begin to relate to it. We often attract a teacher, a friend, a class or workshop or a book to ourselves that begins to awaken new ways to approach the dissolving of the problem.

My awakening began with a chance remark of a friend who had been told about a meeting. My friend did not go, but something within me responded, and I went. That little meeting was the first step on my pathway of unfoldment. I didn't recognize the significance of it until some time later.

Often our reaction to this first stage is to think the approach is silly, or that it doesn't make sense. Perhaps it seems too easy, or unacceptable to our thinking. We don't want to do it. Our resistance comes up very strong. We may even feel angry about the thought of doing it.

Such a reaction is very good, if we can understand that it is the first step in our healing process.

I tell people that any reaction they may feel is there to show them they are already in the process of healing even though the total healing is not yet completed. The truth is the process begins the moment we begin to think about making a change.

Impatience is only another form of resistance. It is resistance to learning and to changing. When we demand that it be done right now, completed at once, then we don't give ourselves time to learn the lesson involved with the problem we have created.

If you want to move to another room, you have to get up and move step by step in that direction. Just sitting in your chair and demanding that you be in the other room will not work. It's the same thing. We all want our problem to be over with, but we don't want to do the small things that will add up to the solution.

Now is the time to acknowledge our responsibility in having created the situation or condition. I'm not talking about having guilt, nor about being a "bad person" for being where you are. I am saying to acknowledge the "power within you" that transforms our every thought into experience. In the past we unknowingly used this power to create things we did not want to experience. We were not aware of what we were doing. Now, by acknowledging our responsibility, we *become* aware and learn to use this power consciously in positive ways for our benefit.

Often when I suggest a solution to the client — a new way to approach a matter or forgiving the person involved — I will see the jaw begin to clench and jut out, and arms cross tightly over the chest. Maybe even fists will form. Resistance is coming to the fore, and I know we have hit upon exactly what needs to be done.

We all have lessons to learn. The things that are so difficult for us are only the lessons we have chosen for ourselves. If things are easy for us, then they are not lessons but are things we already know.

Lessons Can be Learned Through Awareness

If you think of the hardest thing for you to do and how much you resist it, then you're looking at your greatest lesson at the moment. Surrendering, giving up the resistance, and allowing yourself to learn what you need to learn, will make the next step even easier. Don't let your resistance stop you from making the changes. We can work on two levels: 1) Looking at the resistance and 2) Still making the mental changes. Observe yourself, watch how you resist, and then go ahead anyway.

Non-Verbal Clues

Our actions often show our resistance. For instance:
Changing the subject.
Leaving the room.
Going to the bathroom.
Being late.
Getting sick.
Procrastinating by:
Doing something else.
Doing busy work.
Wasting time.
Looking away, or out the window.
Flipping through a magazine.
Refusing to pay attention.
Eating, drinking or smoking.
Creating or ending a relationship.
Creating breakdowns; cars, appliances, plumbing, etc.

Assumptions

We often assume things about others to justify our resistance. We make statements like:
It wouldn't do any good anyway.
My husband/wife won't understand.
I would have to change my whole personality.
Only crazy people go to therapists.
They couldn't help me with my problem.
They couldn't handle my anger.
My case is different.

I don't want to bother them.
It will work itself out.
Nobody else does it.

Beliefs

We grow up with beliefs that become our resistance to changing.
Some of our limiting ideas are:
It's not done.
It's just not right.
It's not right for me to do that.
That wouldn't be spiritual.
Spiritual people don't get angry.
Men/women just don't do that.
My family never did that.
Love is not for me.
That's just silly.
It's too far to drive.
It's too much work.
It's too expensive.
It will take too long.
I don't believe in it.
I'm not that kind of person.

Them

We give our power to others and use that excuse as our resis-
tance to changing. We have ideas like:
God doesn't approve.
I'm waiting for the stars to say it's okay.
This isn't the right environment.
They won't let me change.
I don't have the right teacher/book/class/tools.
My doctor doesn't want me to.
I can't get time off work.
I don't want to be under their spell.

It's all their fault.
They have to change first.
As soon as I get _____ , I'll do it.
You/they don't understand.
I don't want to hurt them.
It's against my upbringing, religion, philosophy.

Self Concepts

We have ideas about ourselves that we use as limitations or resistance to changing. We are:
Too old.
Too young.
Too fat.
Too thin.
Too short.
Too tall.
Too lazy.
Too strong.
Too weak.
Too dumb.
Too smart.
Too poor.
Too worthless.
Too frivolous.
Too serious.
Too stuck.
Maybe it's just all too much.

Delaying Tactics

Our resistance often expresses itself as delaying tactics. We use excuses like:
I'll do it later.
I can't think right now.
I don't have the time right now.

It would take too much time away from my work.
Yes, that's a good good idea. I'll do it some other time.
I have too many other things to do.
I'll think about it tomorrow.
As soon as I get through with _____ .
As soon as I get back from this trip.
The time isn't right.
It's too late, or too soon.

Denial

This form of resistance shows up in denial of the need to do any changing. Things like:
There is nothing wrong with me.
I can't do anything about this problem.
I was all right last time.
What good would it do to change?
If I ignore it, maybe the problem will go away.

Fear

By far the biggest category of resistance is fear — fear of the unknown. Listen to these:
I'm not ready yet.
I might fail.
They might reject me.
What would the neighbors think?
I don't want to open that can of worms.
I'm afraid to tell my husband/wife.
I don't know enough.
I might get hurt.
I may have to change.
It might cost me money.
I would rather die first, or get a divorce first.
I don't want anyone to know I have a problem.
I'm afraid to express my feelings.

I don't want to talk about it.
I don't have the energy.
Who knows where I might end up?
I may lose my freedom.
It's too hard to do.
I don't have enough money now.
I might hurt my back.
I wouldn't be perfect.
I might lose my friends.
I don't trust anyone.
It might hurt my image.
I'm not good enough.

And on and on the list goes. Do you recognize some of these as the ways *you* resist? Look for the resistance in these examples.

A client came to me because she was in a lot of pain. She had broken her back, her neck, and her knee in three separate auto accidents. Yet she was late, got lost, and then was stuck in traffic.

It was easy for her to tell me all her problems, but the minute I said, "Let me talk for a moment," all sorts of turmoil began. Her contact lenses began to bother her. She wanted to sit in another chair. She had to go to the bathroom. Then her lenses had to come out. I could not keep her attention for the rest of the session.

It was all resistance. She wasn't ready to let go and be healed. I discovered her sister also had broken her back twice, and so had her mother.

Another client was an actor, a mime, a street performer, and quite good at it. He bragged about how clever he was at cheating others, especially institutions. He knew how to get away with almost anything, and yet he got away with nothing. He was always broke, at least a month behind in the rent, often without a telephone. His clothes were tacky, work was very sporadic, he had lots of pains in his body, and his love life was zilch.

His theory was that he couldn't stop cheating until some good came into his life. Of course, with what he was giving out, no good could come into his life. He had to stop cheating first.

His resistance was that he was not ready to let go of the old ways.

Leave Your Friends Alone

Too often instead of working on our own changes, we decide which of our friends needs to change. This too is resistance.

In the early days of my work, I had a client who would send me to all her friends in the hospital. Instead of sending them flowers, she would have me go to fix up their problems. I would arrive with my tape recorder in hand, usually finding someone in bed who didn't know why I was there or understand what I was doing. This was before I learned never to work with anyone unless he or she requested it.

Sometimes clients come to me because a friend has given them a session as a present. This usually doesn't work too well, and they seldom come back for further work.

When something works well for us we often want to share it with others. But they may not be ready to make a change at that point in time and space. It's hard enough to make changes when we want to, but to try to make someone else change when he or she doesn't want to is impossible, and it can ruin a good friendship. I push my clients because they come to me. I leave my friends alone.

Mirror Work

Mirrors reflect back to us our feelings about ourselves. They show us clearly the areas to be changed if we want to have a joyous, fulfilling life.

I ask people to look in their eyes and say something positive about themselves every time they pass a mirror. The most powerful way to do affirmations is to look in a mirror and say them out loud. You are immediately aware of the resistance and can move through it quicker. It's good to have a mirror with you as you read this book. Use it often for affirmations and to check where you are resisting and where you are open and flowing.

Now, look in a mirror and say to yourself, "I am willing to change."

Notice how you feel. If you are hesitant, resistant, or just don't want to change, ask yourself why. What old belief are you holding on to? This is not a time to scold yourself. Just notice what is going on and what belief rises to the surface. That is the one that has been causing you a lot of trouble. Can you recognize where it came from?

When we do our affirmations and they don't feel right or nothing seems to happen, it's so easy to say, "Oh, affirmations don't work." It's not that the affirmations don't work, it's that we need to do another step before we begin affirmations.

Repeated Patterns Show Us Our Needs

For every habit we have, for every experience we go through over and over, for every pattern we repeat, there is a *NEED WITHIN US* for it. The need corresponds to some belief we have. If there were not a need, we wouldn't have it, do it, or be it. There is something within us that needs the fat, the poor relationships, the failures, the cigarettes, the anger, the poverty, the abuse, or whatever there is that's a problem for us.

How many times have we said, "I won't ever do that again!" Then, before the day is up we have the piece of cake, smoke the cigarettes, say hateful things to the ones we love, etc. Then we compound the whole problem by angrily saying to ourselves, "Oh, you have no will power, no discipline. You're just weak." This only adds to the load of guilt we already carry.

It has Nothing to Do With Will Power or Discipline

Whatever we are trying to release in our lives is just a symptom, an outer effect. Trying to eliminate the symptom without working on dissolving the cause is useless. The moment we release our will power or discipline, the symptom crops up again.

Willingness to Release the Need

I say to clients, "There must be a need in you for this condition, or you wouldn't have it. Let's go back a step and work on the *WILLINGNESS TO RELEASE THE NEED*. When the need is gone, you will have no desire for the cigarette or the overeating or the negative pattern."

One of the first affirmations to use is: "I am willing to release the *NEED* for the resistance, or the headache, or the constipation, or the excess weight, or the lack of money or whatever." Say: "I am willing to release the need for . . ." If you are resisting at this point, then your other affirmations cannot work.

The webs we create around ourselves need to be unwound. If you have ever untangled a ball of string, you know that yanking and pulling only makes it worse. You need to very gently and patiently unravel the knots. Be gentle and patient with *yourself* as you untangle your own mental knots. Get help if you need it. Above all, love yourself in the process. The *willingness* to let go of the old is the key. That is the secret.

When I say "needing the problem," I mean that according to our particular set of thought patterns, we "need" to have certain outer effects or experiences. Every outer effect is the natural expression of an inner thought pattern. To battle only the outer effect or symptom is wasted energy and often increases the problem.

"I am Unworthy" Creates Procrastination

If one of my inner belief systems or thought patterns is, "I am unworthy," then one of my outer effects will probably be procrastination. After all, procrastination is one way to keep us from getting where we say we want to go. Most people who procrastinate will spend a lot of time and energy berating themselves for procrastinating. They will call themselves lazy and generally will make themselves out to feel they are "bad persons."

Resentment of Another's Good

I had a client who loved attention and usually came to class late so he could create a stir. He had been the baby of 18 children, and he came last on the list of getting. As a child he watched everyone else have while he just longed for his own. Even now when someone had good fortune, he would not rejoice with them. Instead he would say, "Oh, I wish I had that," or "Oh, why don't I ever get that?"

His resentment of their good was a barrier to his own growth and change.

Self-Worth Opens Many Doors

A client who was 79 came to me. She taught singing, and several of her students were making television commercials. She wanted to do this too, but was afraid. I supported her totally and explained, "There is nobody like you. Just be yourself." I said, "Do it for the fun of it. There are people out there looking for exactly what you have to offer. Let them know you exist."

She called several agents and casting directors, and said, "I am a senior, senior citizen, and I want to do commercials." In a short time she had a commercial, and since then she's never stopped working. I often see her on TV and in magazines. New careers can start at any age, especially when you do it for the fun of it.

Self-Criticizing is Totally Missing the Mark

It will only intensify the procrastination and laziness. The place to put the mental energy is into releasing the old and creating a new thought pattern. Say: *"I am willing to release the need to be unworthy. I am worthy of the very best in life and I now lovingly allow myself to accept it."*

"As I spend a few days doing this affirmation over and over, my outer effect pattern of procrastination will automatically begin to fade."

"As I internally create a pattern of self-worth, then I no longer have the need to delay my good."

Do you see how this could apply to some of the negative patterns or outer effects in your life? Let's stop wasting time and energy putting ourselves down for something we can't help doing if we have certain inner beliefs. *Change the beliefs.*

No matter how you approach it, or what subject matter we are talking about, we are only dealing with thoughts, and thoughts can be changed.

When we want to change a condition, we need to say so.

"I am willing to release the pattern within me that is creating this condition."

You can say this to yourself over and over every time you think of your illness or problem. The minute you say it, you are stepping out of the victim class. You are no longer helpless, you are acknowledging your own power. You are saying, "I am beginning to understand that I created this. I now take my own power back. I am going to release this old idea and let it go."

Self-Criticism

I have a client who will eat a pound of butter and everything else she can get hold of when she cannot bear to be with her own negative thoughts. The next day she will be angry at her body for being heavy. When she was a little girl, she would walk around the family dinner table finishing off everyone's leftovers and eating a whole stick of butter. The family would laugh and think it was cute. It was almost the only approval she got from her family.

When you scold yourself, when you berate yourself, when you "beat yourself up," who do you think you're treating this way?

Almost all of our programming, both negative and positive, was accepted by us by the time we were three years old. Our experiences since then are based upon what we accepted and believed about ourselves and about life at that time. The way we were treated when we were very little is usually the way we treat ourselves now. The person you are scolding is a three year old child within you.

If you are a person who gets angry at yourself for being afraid and fearful, think of yourself as being three years old. If you had a little three year old child in front of you who was afraid, what would you do? Would you be angry at him, or would you reach out your arms and comfort the child until it felt safe and at ease? The adults around you when you were a child may not have known how to comfort you at that time. Now *you* are the adult in your life, and if you're not comforting the child within you, then that is very sad indeed.

What was done in the past is done, and it is over now. But this is present time, and you now have the opportunity to treat yourself the way you wish to be treated. A frightened child needs comforting, not scolding. Scolding yourself only makes you more frightened, and there is nowhere to turn. When the child within feels unsafe, it creates a lot of trouble. Remember how it felt to be belittled when you were young? It feels the same way now to that child within.

Be kind to yourself. Begin to love and approve of yourself. That's what that little child needs in order to express itself at its highest potential.

*In the infinity of life where I am, all is perfect,
whole and complete. I see any resistance patterns within me
only as something else to release.
They have no power over me. I am the power in my world.
I flow with the changes taking place in my life as best I can.
I approve of myself and the way I am changing.
I am doing the best I can. Each day gets easier.
I rejoice that I am in the rhythm and flow
of my ever-changing life.
Today is a wonderful day.
I choose to make it so.
All is well in my world.*

♥ *Chapter Seven*
HOW TO CHANGE

"I cross bridges with joy and with ease."

I love "how to's." All the theory in the world is useless unless we know how to apply it and make a change. I have always been a very pragmatic, practical person with a great need to know how to do things.

The principles we will be working with at this time are:

Nurturing the willingness to let go,

Controlling the mind,

Learning how forgiveness of self and others releases us.

Releasing the Need

Sometimes when we try to release a pattern, the whole situation seems to get worse for a while. This is not a bad thing. It is a sign that the situation is beginning to move. Our affirmations are working, and we need to keep going.

Examples

We are working on increasing prosperity, and we lose our wallet.

We are working on improving our relationships, and we have a fight.

We are working on becoming healthy, and we catch a cold.

We are working on expressing our creative talents and abilities, and we get fired.

Sometimes the problem moves in a different direction, and we begin to see and understand more. For example, let's assume you are trying to give up smoking and you are saying, "I am willing to release the 'need' for cigarettes." As you continue to do this, you notice your relationships becoming more uncomfortable.

Don't despair, this is a sign of the process working.

You might ask yourself a series of questions like, "Am I willing to give up uncomfortable relationships? Were my cigarettes creating a smoke screen so I wouldn't see how uncomfortable these relationships are? Why am I creating these relationships?"

You notice the cigarettes are only a symptom and not a cause. Now you are developing insight and understanding that will set you free.

You begin to say, "I am willing to release the 'need' for uncomfortable relationships."

Then you notice the reason you're so uncomfortable is that other people always seem to be criticizing you.

Being aware that we always create all of our experiences, you now begin to say, "I am willing to release the need to be criticized."

You then think about criticism, and you realize that as a child, you received a lot of criticism. That little kid inside of you only feels "at home" when it is being criticized. Your way of hiding from this had become creating a "smoke screen."

Perhaps you see the next step as affirming, "I am willing to forgive . . ."

As you continue to do your affirmations, you may find that cigarettes no longer attract you and the people in your life no longer criticize you. Then you *know* you have released your need.

This usually takes a little while to work out. If you are gently persisₑant and are willing to give yourself a few quiet moments each day to reflect on your process of change, you will get the answers. The Intelligence within you is the same Intelligence that created this entire planet. Trust your Inner Guidance to reveal to you whatever it is you need to know.

Exercise: Releasing the Need

In a workshop situation, I would have you do this exercise with a partner. However, you can do it equally as well using a mirror, a big one, if possible.

Think for a moment about something in your life you want to change. Go to the mirror and look into your eyes and say out loud, "I now realize that I have created this condition, and I am now willing to release the pattern in my consciousness that is responsible for this condition." Say it several times, with feeling.

If you were with a partner, I would have your partner tell you if they really thought you meant it. I would want you to *convince* your partner.

Ask yourself if you really mean it. Convince yourself in the mirror that this time you *are* ready to step out of the bondage of the past.

At this point many people get scared because they don't know *HOW* to do this releasing. They are afraid to commit themselves until they know all the answers. It's only more resistance. Just pass through it.

One of the great things is that we do not have to know how. All we need is to be willing. The Universal Intelligence or your subconscious mind will figure out the hows. Every thought you think and every word you speak is being responded to, and the point of power is in this moment. The thoughts you are thinking and the words you are declaring at this moment are creating your future.

Your Mind is a Tool

You are much more than your mind. You may think your mind is running the show. But that is only because you have trained your mind to think in this way. You can also untrain and retrain this tool of yours.

Your mind is a tool for you to use in any way you wish. The way you now use your mind is only a habit, and habits, any habits, can be changed if we want to do so, or even if we only know it is possible to do so.

Quiet the chatter of your mind for a moment and really think about this concept: *YOUR MIND IS A TOOL YOU CAN CHOOSE TO USE ANY WAY YOU WISH.*

The thoughts you "choose" to think create the experiences you have. If you believe that it is hard or difficult to change a habit or a thought, then your choice of this thought will make it true for you. If you would choose to think, "It is becoming easier for me to make changes," then your choice of this thought will make that true for you.

Controlling the Mind

There is an incredible power and intelligence within you constantly responding to your thoughts and words. As you learn to control your mind by the conscious choice of thoughts, you align yourself with this power.

Do not think your mind is in control. *You* are in control of your mind. *You* use your mind. You *can* stop thinking those old thoughts.

When your old thinking tries to come back and say, "It's so hard to change," take mental control. Say to your mind, "I now choose to believe it is becoming easier for me to make changes." You may have to have this conversation with your mind several times for it to acknowledge that you are in control and that what you say goes.

The Only Thing You Ever Have Any Control of is Your Current Thought

Your old thoughts are gone; there is nothing you can do about them except live out the experiences they caused. Your future thoughts have not been formed, and you do not know what they will be. Your current thought, the one you are thinking right now, is totally under your control.

Example

If you have a little child who has been allowed to stay up as late as he wishes for a long time, and then you make a decision that you now want this child to go to bed at 8:00 every night, what do you think the first night will be like?

The child will rebel against this new rule and may kick and scream and do its best to stay out of bed. If you relent at *this* time, the child wins and will try to control you forever.

However, if you calmly stick to your decision and firmly insist that this is the new bedtime, the rebelling will get less and less. In two or three nights, the new routine will be established.

It is the same thing with your mind. Of course it will rebel at first. It does not want to be retrained. But you are in control, and if you stay focused and firm, in a very short time the new way of thinking will be established. And you will feel so good to realize that *you are not a helpless victim of your own thoughts, but rather a master of your own mind.*

Exercise: Letting Go

As you read this, take a deep breath and, as you exhale, allow all the tension to leave your body. Let your scalp and your forehead and your face relax. Your head does not need to be tense in order for you to read. Let your tongue and your throat and your shoulders relax. You can hold a book with relaxed arms and hands. Do that now. Let your back and your abdomen and your pelvis relax. Let your breathing be at peace as you relax your legs and feet.

Is there a big change in your body since you began the previous paragraph? Notice how much you hold on. If you are doing it with your body, you are doing it with your mind.

In this relaxed, comfortable position, say to yourself, "I am willing to let go. I release. I let go. I release all tension. I release all fear. I release all anger. I release all guilt. I release all sadness. I let go of all old limitations. I let go, and I am at peace. I am at peace with myself. I am at peace with the process of life. I am safe."

Go over this exercise two or three times. Feel the ease of letting go. Repeat it whenever you feel thoughts of difficulty coming up. It takes a little practice for the routine to become a part of you. When you put yourself into this peaceful state first, it becomes easy for your affirmations to take hold. You become open and receptive to them. There is no need to struggle or stress or strain. Just relax and think the appropriate thoughts. Yes, it is this easy.

Physical Releasing

Sometimes we need to experience a physical letting go. Experiences and emotions can get locked in the body. Screaming in the car with all the windows rolled up can be very releasing if we have been stifling our verbal expression. Beating the bed or kicking pillows is a harmless way to release pent-up anger, as is playing tennis or running.

A while ago I had a pain in my shoulder for a day or two. I tried to ignore it, but it wouldn't go away. Finally, I sat down and asked myself, "What is happening here? What am I feeling?"

"It feels like burning. Burning . . . burning . . . that means anger. What are you angry about?"

I couldn't think what I was angry about, so I said, "Well, let's see if we can find out." I put two large pillows on the bed and began to hit them with a lot of energy.

After about twelve hits, I realized exactly what I was angry about. It was so clear. So I beat the pillows even harder and made some noise and released the emotions from my body. When I got through, I felt much better, and the next day my shoulder was fine.

Letting the Past Hold you Back

Many people come to me and say *they cannot enjoy today because of something that happened in the past.* Because they did not do something or do it in a certain way in the past, they cannot live a full life today. Because they no longer have something they had in the past, they cannot enjoy today. Because they were hurt in the past, they will not accept love now. Because something unpleasant happened when they did something once, they are sure it will happen again today. Because they once did something that they are sorry for, they are sure they are bad people forever. Because once someone did something to them, it is now all the other person's fault that their life is not where they want it to be. Because they became angry over a situation in the past, they will hold on to that self-righteousness. Because of some very old experience where they were treated badly, they will never forgive and forget.

Because I did not get invited to the High School Prom, I cannot enjoy life today.

Because I did poorly at my first audition, I will be terrified of auditions forever.

Because I am no longer married, I cannot live a full life today.

Because my first relationship ended, I can no longer be open to love.

Because I was hurt by a remark once, I will never trust anyone again.

Because I stole something once, I must punish myself forever.

Because I was poor as a child, I will never get anywhere.

What we often refuse to realize is that holding onto the past — no matter what it was or how awful it was, is *ONLY HURTING US.* "They" really don't care. Usually "they" are not even aware. We are only hurting ourselves by refusing to live in this moment to the fullest.

The past is over and done and cannot be changed. This is the only moment we can experience. Even when we grudge about the past, we are experiencing our memory of it in this moment, and losing the real experience of this moment in the process.

Exercise: Releasing

Let us now clean up the past in our minds. Release the emotional attachment to it. Allow the memories to be just memories.

If you think back to what you used to wear in the third grade, usually there is no emotional attachment. It's just a memory.

It can be the same for all of the past events in our lives. As we let go, we become free to use all of our mental power to enjoy this moment and to create a great future.

List all the things you are willing to let go of. How willing are you to do this? Notice your reactions. What will you have to do to let these things go? How willing are you to do so? What is your resistance level?

Forgiveness

Next step. *Forgiveness.* Forgiveness of ourselves and of others releases us from the past. The *Course In Miracles* says over and over that forgiveness is the answer to almost everything. I know that when we are stuck, it usually means there is some more forgiving to be done. When we do not flow freely with life in the present moment, it usually means we are holding on to a past moment. It can be regret, sadness, hurt, fear or guilt, blame, anger, resentment and sometimes even the desire for revenge. *Each one of these states comes from a space of unforgiveness, a refusal to let go and come into the present moment.*

Love is always the answer to healing of any sort. And the pathway to love is forgiveness. Forgiveness dissolves resentment. There are several ways I approach this.

Exercise: Dissolving Resentment

There is an old Emmet Fox exercise for dissolving resentment that always works. He recommends that you sit quietly, close your eyes and allow your mind and body to relax. Then imagine yourself sitting in a darkened theatre, and in front of you is a small stage. On that stage place the person you resent the most. It could be past or present, living or dead. When you see this person clearly, visualize good things happening to this person. Things that would be meaningful to them. See them smiling and happy.

Hold this image for a few minutes, then let it fade away. I like to add another step. As they leave the stage, put yourself up there. See good things happening to you. See yourself smiling and happy. Be aware that the abundance of the Universe is available for all of us.

The above exercise dissolves the dark clouds of resentment most of us carry. For some, it will be very difficult to do. Each time you do it, you may get a different person. Do it once a day for a month and notice how much lighter you feel.

Exercise: Revenge

Those on the spiritual pathway know the importance of forgiveness. For some of us, there is a step that is necessary before we can totally forgive. Sometimes the little kid in us needs to have revenge before it is free to forgive. For that, this exercise is very helpful.

Close your eyes, sit quietly and peacefully. Think of the person who is hardest to forgive. What would you really like to do to them? What do they need to do to get your forgiveness? Imagine that happening now. Get into the details. How long do you want them to suffer or do penance?

When you feel complete, condense time and let it be over forever. Usually at this point you feel lighter, and it is easier to think about forgiveness. To indulge in this every day would not be good for you. To do it once as a closing exercise can be freeing.

Exercise: Forgiveness

Now we are ready to forgive. Do this exercise with a partner if you can, or do it out loud if you are alone.

Again sit quietly with your eyes closed and say, "The person I need to forgive is _____ and I forgive you for _____."

Do this over and over. You will have many things to forgive some for and only one or two to forgive others for. If you have a partner, let them say to you, "Thank you, I

set you free now." If you do not, then imagine the person
you are forgiving saying it to you. Do this for at least five
or ten minutes. Search your heart for the injustices you still
carry. Then let them go.

When you have cleared as much as you can for now,
turn your attention to yourself. Say out loud to yourself, "I
forgive myself for _____ ." Do this for another five minutes
or so. These are powerful exercises and good to do at least
once a week to clear out any remaining rubbish. Some
experiences are easy to let go and some we have to chip
away at, until suddenly one day they let go and dissolve.

Exercise: Visualization

Another good exercise. Have someone read this one to
you if you can, or put it on tape and listen to it.

Begin to visualize yourself as a little child of five or six.
Look deeply into this little child's eyes. See the longing
that is there and realize that there is only one thing this
little child wants from you, and that is love. So reach out
your arms and embrace this child. Hold it with love and
tenderness. Tell it how much you love it, how much you
care. Admire everything about this child and say that it's
okay to make mistakes while learning. Promise that you
will always be there no matter what. Now let this little
child get very small, until it is just the size to fit into your
heart. Put it there so whenever you look down you can see
this little face looking up at you and you can give it lots of
love.

Now visualize your mother as a little girl of four or five,
frightened and looking for love and not knowing where to
find it. Reach out your arms and hold this little girl and let
her know how much you love her, how much you care. Let
her know she can rely on you to always be there, no matter
what. When she quiets down and begins to feel safe, let her
get very small, just the size to fit into your heart. Put her
there with your own little child. Let them give each other
lots of love.

Now imagine your father as a little boy of three or four, frightened, crying and looking for love. See the tears rolling down his little face as he doesn't know where to turn. You have become good at comforting frightened little children, so reach out your arms and hold his trembling little body. Comfort him. Croon to him. Let him feel how much you love him. Let him feel that you will always be there for him.

When his tears are dry, and you feel the love and peace in his little body, let him get very small, just the size to fit into your heart. Put him there so those three little children can give each other lots of love and you can love them all.

* * *

There is so much love in your heart that you could heal the entire planet. But just for now let us use this love to heal you. Feel a warmth beginning to glow in your heart center, a softness, a gentleness. Let this feeling begin to change the way you think and talk about yourself.

In the infinity of life where I am,
all is perfect, whole and complete.
Change is the natural law of my life. I welcome change.
I am willing to change. I choose to change my thinking.
I choose to change the words I use.
I move from the old to the new with ease and with joy.
It is easier for me to forgive than I thought.
Forgiving makes me feel free and light.
It is with joy that I learn to love myself more and more.
The more resentment I release,
the more love I have to express.
Changing my thoughts makes me feel good.
I am learning to choose to make today a pleasure to experience.
All is well in my world.

💟 *Chapter Eight*

BUILDING THE NEW

"The answers within me come to my
awareness with ease."

I don't want to be fat.
I don't want to be broke.
I don't want to be old.
I don't want to live here.
I don't want to have this relationship.
I don't want to be like my mother/father.
I don't want to be stuck in this job.
I don't want to have this hair/nose/body.
I don't want to be lonely.
I don't want to be unhappy.
I don't want to be sick.

What You Put Your Attention on Grows

The above shows how we are culturally taught to fight the negative mentally — thinking that if we do so, the positive will automatically come to us. It doesn't work that way.

How often have you lamented about what you didn't want? Did it ever bring you what you really wanted? Fighting the negative is a total waste of time if you really want to make changes in your life. *The more you dwell on what you don't want, the more of it you create. The things about yourself or your life that you have always disliked are probably still with you.*

What you put your attention on grows and becomes permanent in your life. Move away from the negative and put your attention on what it is that you really *do* want to be or have. Let's turn the above negative affirmations into positive affirmations.

I am slender.
I am prosperous.
I am eternally young.
I now move to a better place.
I have a wonderful new relationship.
I am my own person.
I love my hair/nose/body.
I am filled with love and affection.
I am joyous and happy and free.
I am totally healthy.

Affirmations

Learn to think in positive affirmations. Affirmations are any statements you make. Too often we think in negative affirmations. Negative affirmations only create more of what you say you don't want. Saying, "I hate my job," will get you nowhere. Declaring, "I now accept a wonderful new job," will open the channels in your consciousness to create that.

Continuously make positive statements about how you want your life to be. However, there is one point that is very important in this: *Always make your statements in PRESENT TENSE,* such as, "I am" or "I have." Your subconscious mind is such an obedient servant that if you declare in future tense, "I want," or "I will have," then that is where it will always stay — just out of your reach in the future!

The Process of Loving the Self

As I have said before, no matter what the problem, the main issue to work on is *LOVING THE SELF*. This is the "magic wand" that dissolves problems. Remember the times when you have felt good about yourself and how well your life was going? Remember the times when you were in love and for those periods you seemed to have no problems? Well, loving yourself is going to bring such a surge of good feelings and good fortune to you that you will be dancing on air. *LOVING YOURSELF MAKES YOU FEEL GOOD.*

It is impossible to really love yourself unless you have self-approval and self-acceptance. This means no criticism whatsoever. I can hear all the objections right now.

"But I have always criticized myself."

"How can I possibly like that about myself?"

"My parents/teachers/lovers always criticized me."

"How will I be motivated?"

"But it is wrong for me to do those things."

"How am I going to change if I don't criticize myself?"

Training the Mind

Self-criticism like the above is just the mind going on with old chatter. See how you have trained your mind to berate you and be resistant to change? Ignore those thoughts and get on with the important work at hand!

Let's go back to an exercise we did earlier. Look into the mirror again and say, "I love and approve of myself exactly as I am."

How does that feel now? Is it a little easier after the forgiveness work we have done? This is still the main issue. Self-approval and self-acceptance are the keys to positive changes.

In the days when my own self-denial was so prevalent, I would occasionally slap my own face. I didn't know the meaning of self-acceptance. My belief in my own lacks and limitations was stronger than anything anyone else could say to the contrary. If someone told me I was loved, my immediate reaction was, "Why? What could anyone possibly see in me?" Or the classic thought, "If they only knew what I was *really* like inside, they wouldn't love me."

I was not aware that all good begins with accepting that which is within one's self, and loving that self which is you. It took quite a while to develop a peaceful, loving relationship with *myself.*

First I used to hunt for the little things about myself I thought
were "good qualities." Even this helped, and my own health began
to improve. Good health begins with loving the self. So do prosperity and love and creative self-expression. Later I learned to
love and approve of all of me, even those qualities I thought
were "not good enough." That was when I really began to make
progress.

Exercise: I Approve of Myself

I have given this exercise to hundreds of people, and the
results are phenomenal. For the next month say over and
over to yourself, *"I APPROVE OF MYSELF."*

Do this three or four hundred times a day, at least. No,
it's not too many times. When you are worrying, you go
over your problem at least that many times. Let "I approve
of myself" become a walking mantra, something you just
say over and over and over to yourself, almost nonstop.

Saying "I approve of myself" is guaranteed to bring up
everything buried in your consciousnes that is in opposition.

When the negative thought comes up like, "How can
you approve of yourself when you are fat?" or "It's silly to
think this can do any good," or "You are no good," or
whatever your negative babble will be, *this* is the time to
take mental control. Give it no importance. Just see the
thought for what it is, another way to keep you stuck in the
past. Gently say to this thought, "I let you go, I approve of
myself."

Even considering doing this exercise can bring up a lot
of stuff, like "It feels silly," "It doesn't feel true," "It's a
lie," "It sounds stuck up," or "How can I approve of myself
when I do that?"

Let them all just pass through. These are only resistance
thoughts. They have no power over you unless you choose
to believe them.

"I approve of myself, I approve of myself, I approve of
myself." No matter what happens, no matter who says
what to you, no matter who does what to you, just keep it

going. In fact, when you can say that to yourself when
someone is doing something you don't approve of, you will
know you are growing and changing.

Thoughts have no power over us unless we give in to them.
Thoughts are only words strung together. They have *NO MEAN-
ING WHATSOEVER.* Only *we* give meaning to them. And *we*
choose what sort of meaning we give to them. Let us choose to
think thoughts that nourish and support us.

Part of self-acceptance is releasing other people's opinions. If I
were with you and kept telling you, "You are a purple pig, you are
a purple pig." You would either laugh at me, or get annoyed
with me and think I was crazy. It would be most unlikely you
would think it was true. Yet many of the things we have chosen to
believe about ourselves are just as far out and untrue. To believe
that your self-worth is dependent on the shape of your body is your
version of believing that "You are a purple pig."

*Often what we think of as the things "wrong" with us are only
our expressions of our own individuality.* This is our uniqueness
and what is special about us. Nature never repeats itself. Since
time began on this planet, there have never been two snowflakes
alike nor two raindrops the same. And every daisy is different from
every other daisy. Our fingerprints are different, and we are different. *We are meant to be different. When we can accept this,
then there is no competition and no comparison.* To try to be like
another is to shrivel our soul. We have come to this planet to
express who *we are.*

I didn't even know who I was until I began to learn to love
myself as I am in this moment.

Put Your Awareness Into Practice

Think thoughts that make you happy. Do things that make you
feel good. Be with people who make you feel good. Eat things that
make your body feel good. Go at a pace that makes you feel good.

Planting Seeds

Think for a moment of a tomato plant. A healthy plant can have over a hundred tomatoes on it. In order to get this tomato plant with all these tomatoes on it, we need to start with a small dried seed. That seed doesn't look like a tomato plant. It sure doesn't taste like a tomato plant. If you didn't know for sure, you would not even believe it could be a tomato plant. However, let's say you plant this seed in fertile soil and you water it and let the sun shine on it.

When the first little tiny shoot comes up, you don't stomp on it and say, "That's not a tomato plant." Rather, you look at it and say, "Oh boy! Here it comes," and you watch it grow with delight. In time, if you continue to water it and give it lots of sunshine and pull away any weeds, you might have a tomato plant with more than a hundred luscious tomatoes. It all began with that one tiny seed.

It is the same with creating a new experience for yourself. The soil you plant in is your subconscious mind. The seed is the new affirmation. *The whole new experience is in this tiny seed.* You water it with affirmations. You let the sunshine of positive thoughts beam on it. You weed the garden by pulling out the negative thoughts that come up. And when you first see the tiniest little evidence, you don't stomp on it and say, "That's not enough!" Instead, you look at this first breakthrough and say with glee, "Oh boy! Here it comes! It's working!"

Then you watch it grow and become your desire in manifestation.

Exercise: Create New Changes

Now is the time to *take your list of things that are wrong with you and turn them into positive affirmations.* Or you can list all the changes you want to make and have and do. Then select three from this list and turn them into positive affirmations.

Say your negative list was something like this:
My life is a mess.

I should lose weight.
Nobody loves me.
I want to move.
I hate my job.
I should get organized.
I don't do enough.
I'm not good enough.
You can then turn them around to something like this:
I am willing to release the pattern in me that created
these conditions.
I am in the process of positive changes.
I have a happy, slender body.
I experience love wherever I go.
I have the perfect living space.
I now create a wonderful new job.
I am now very well organized.
I appreciate all that I do.
I love and approve of myself.
I trust the process of life to bring me my highest good.
I deserve the best, and I accept it now.

Out of this group of affirmations will come all the things
you want to change on your list. Loving and approving of
yourself, creating a space of safety, trusting and deserving
and accepting will enable your body weight to normalize.
They will create organization in your mind, create loving
relationships in your life, attract a new job and a new place
to live. It is miraculous the way a tomato plant grows. It is
miraculous the way we can demonstrate our desires.

Deserving Your Good

Do you believe you deserve to have what you desire? If you
don't, you won't allow yourself to have it. Circumstances beyond
your control will crop up to frustrate you.

Exercise: I Deserve

Look in your mirror again and say, "I deserve to have/or
be ... and I accept it now." Say it two or three times.
How do you feel? Always pay attention to your feelings,

to what is going on in your body. Does it feel true, or do you still feel unworthy?

If you have any negative feelings in your body, then go back to affirming, "I release the pattern in my consciousness that is creating resistance to my good." "I deserve . . ."

Repeat this until you get the acceptance feelings, even if you have to do it several days in a row.

Holistic Philosophy

In our approach to Building the New, we want to use a holistic approach. The holistic philosophy is to nurture and nourish the entire being — the Body, the Mind, and the Spirit. If we ignore any of these areas, we are incomplete, we lack wholeness. It doesn't matter where we start as long as we also include the other areas.

If we begin with the body, we would want to work with nutrition, to learn the relationship between our choice of food and beverages, and how they affect the way we feel. We want to make the best choices for our body. There are herbs and vitamins, Homeopathy and Bach Flower Remedies. We might explore Colonics.

We would want to find a form of exercise that appeals to us. Exercise is something that strengthens our bones and keeps our bodies young. In addition to sports and swimming, consider dancing, Tai-Chi, martial arts, and Yoga. I love my trampoline and use it daily. My slant board enhances my periods of relaxation.

We might want to explore some form of body work such as Rolfing, Heller Work or Trager. Massage, Foot Reflexology, Acupuncture or Chiropractic work are all beneficial. There are also the Alexander Method, Bioenergetics, Feldenkrais, Touch for Health, and Reiki forms of body work.

With the mind we could explore visualization techniques, guided imagery, and affirmations. There are lots of psychological techniques: Gestalt, Hypnosis, Re-birthing, Psycho Drama, Past-Life Regressions, Art Therapy, even Dream Work.

Meditation in any of its forms is a wonderful way to quiet the mind and allow your own "knowingness" to come to the surface. I usually just sit with my eyes closed and say, "What is it I need to know?" and then wait quietly for an answer. If the answer comes, fine; if it doesn't, fine. It will come another day.

There are *groups* that do workshops for all different tastes such as Insight, Loving Relationships Training, est, Advocate Experience, the Ken Keyes group, Actualizations, and many more. Many of these groups do weekend workshops. These weekends give you a chance to see a whole new viewpoint about life just as my own weekend workshops do. No one workshop will totally clear up *ALL* your problems forever. However, they can assist you in changing your life in the here and now.

In the Spiritual Realm there is prayer, there is meditation, and becoming connected with your Higher Source. Practicing forgiveness and unconditional love to me are spiritual practices.

There are many spiritual groups. In addition to the Christian churches there are Metaphysical churches, like Religious Science and Unity. There are the Self-Realization Fellowship, M.S.I.A., Transcendental Meditation, the Siddha Foundation, etc.

I want you to know that there are many, many avenues you can explore. If one way doesn't work for you, try another. All these suggestions have proved to be beneficial. I cannot say which one is right for you. That is something you will have to discover for yourself. No one method or one person or one group has all the answers for everyone. I don't have all the answers for everyone. I am just one more stepping stone on the pathway to holistic health.

In the infinity of life where I am, all is perfect,
whole and complete. My life is ever new.
Each moment of my life is new and fresh and vital.
I use my affirmative thinking to create exactly what I want.
This is a new day. I am a new me.
I think differently. I speak differently. I act differently.
Others treat me differently.
My new world is a reflection of my new thinking.
It is a joy and a delight to plant new seeds,
for I know these seeds will become my new experiences.
All is well in my world.

♥ Chapter Nine
DAILY WORK

"I enjoy practicing my new mental skills."

If a Child Gave up at the First Fall, It Would Never Learn to Walk

Like any other new thing you are learning, it takes practice to make it part of your life. First there is a lot of concentration, and some of us choose to make this "hard work." I don't like to think of it as hard work, but rather as something new to learn.

The process of learning is always the same no matter what the subject — whether you're learning to drive a car, or type, or play tennis, or think in a positive manner. First, we fumble and bumble as our subconscious mind learns by trial and yet, every time we come back to our practicing it gets easier, and we do it a little better. Of course, you won't be "perfect" the first day. You will be doing whatever you can do. That's good enough for a start.

Say to yourself often, "I'm doing the best I can."

Always Support Yourself

I well remember my first lecture. When I came down from the podium, I immediately said to myself, "Louise, you were wonderful. You were absolutely fantastic for the first time. When you have done five or six of these, you will be a pro."

A couple of hours later, I said to myself, "I think we could change a few things. Let's adjust this, and let's adjust that." I refused to criticize myself in any way.

If I had come off the podium and begun berating myself with, "Oh, you were so awful. You made this mistake, and you made that mistake," then I would have dreaded my second lecture. As it was, the second one was better than the first, and by the sixth one, I was feeling like a pro.

Seeing "The Law" Working All Around Us

Just before I began writing this book, I bought myself a word processor computer. I called her my "Magic Lady." It was something new I chose to learn. I discovered that learning the computer was very much like learning the Spiritual Laws. When I learned the computer's laws, then she did indeed perform "magic" for me. When I did not follow her laws to the letter, then either nothing would happen or it would not work the way *I* wanted it to work. She would not give an inch. I could get as frustrated as I wanted while she patiently waited for me to learn her laws, and then she gave me magic. It took practice.

It's the same with the work you're learning to do now. You must learn the Spiritual Laws and follow them to the letter. You cannot bend them to your old way of thinking. You must learn and follow the new language, and when you do, *then* "magic" will be demonstrated in your life.

Reinforce Your Learning

The more ways you can reinforce your new learning the better. I suggest:

Expressing Gratitude
Writing Affirmations
Sitting in Meditation
Enjoying Exercise
Practicing Good Nutrition
Doing Affirmations Aloud

Singing Affirmations
Taking Time for Relaxation Exercises
Using Visualization, Mental Imagery
Reading and Study

My Daily Work

My own daily work goes something like this.

My first thoughts on awakening before I open my eyes are to be thankful for everything I can think of.

After a shower I take half an hour or so to meditate and do my affirmations and prayers.

Then about 15 minutes of exercise, usually on the trampoline. Sometimes I join the 6:00 a.m. TV aerobic program on television.

Now I'm ready for breakfast consisting of fruit and fruit juices and herbal tea. I thank the Earth Mother for providing this food for me, and I thank the food for giving its life to nourish me.

Before lunch I like to go to a mirror and do some affirmations out loud, I may even sing them.

Something like:

Louise, you are wonderful and I love you.
This is one of the best days of your life.
Everything is working out for your highest good.
Whatever you need to know is revealed to you.
Whatever you need comes to you.
All is well.

Lunch is often a large salad. Again the food is blessed and thanked.

In the late afternoon I spend a few minutes on my slant board allowing my body to experience some deep relaxation. I may listen to a tape at this time.

Dinner will be steamed vegetables and a grain. Sometimes I'll eat fish or chicken. My body works best on simple food. I like to share dinner with others, and we bless each other in addition to the food.

Sometimes in the evening I take a few moments to read and study. There is always more to learn. At this time I may also write out my current affirmation 10 or 20 times.

As I go to bed I collect my thoughts. I go over the day and bless each activity. I affirm that I will sleep deeply and soundly, awakening in the morning bright and refreshed and looking forward to the new day.

Sounds overwhelming, doesn't it? To begin with, it seems like a lot to cope with, but after a short period of time your new way of thinking will become as much a part of your life as bathing or brushing your teeth. You will do it automatically and easily.

It would be wonderful for a family in the morning to do some of these things together. Meditating together in the morning to start the day or just before dinner brings peace and harmony to all. If you think you don't have the time, you might get up half an hour earlier. The benefits would be well worth the effort.

How Do You Begin Your Day?

What is the first thing you say in the morning when you wake up? We all have something we say almost every day. Is it positive or negative? I can remember when I used to awaken in the morning and say with a groan, *"OH GOD, ANOTHER DAY."* And that is exactly the sort of day I would have, one thing after another going wrong. Now when I awaken and before I even open my eyes, I thank the bed for a good night's sleep. After all, we have spent the whole night together in comfort. Then with my eyes still closed, I spend about ten minutes just being thankful for all the good in my life. I program my day a bit, affirming that everything will go well and that I will enjoy it all. This is before I get up and do my morning mediation or prayers.

Meditation

Give yourself a few minutes every day to sit in quiet *meditation.* If you are new at meditation, begin with five minutes. Sit quietly, observe your breathing and allow the thoughts to pass gently through your mind. Give them no importance and they will pass on. It is the nature of the mind to think, so don't try to get rid of thoughts.

There are many classes and books you can explore to find ways to meditate. No mattter how or where you begin, you will eventually create the method best for you. I usually just sit quietly and ask, "What is it that I need to know?" I allow the answer to come if it wants to, if not, I know it will come later. There is no right or wrong way to meditate.

Another form of meditation is to sit quietly and observe the breath as it goes in and out of your body. As you inhale count one, as you exhale count two. Continue counting until you get to 10, then begin again at one. If you find your mind doing the laundry list, begin again at one. If you notice your counting takes you to 25 or so, just go back to one.

There was one client who seemed to me to be so bright and intelligent. Her mind was unusually clever and quick, and she had a great sense of humor. Yet she could not get her act together. She was overweight, broke, frustrated in her career and without a romance for many years. She could accept all the metaphysical concepts quickly, they made a lot of sense to her. Yet she was too clever, too quick. She found it difficult to slow herself down enough to practice over a meaningful period of time the ideas she could grasp so quickly on a moment-by-moment basis.

Daily meditation helped her enormously. We began with only five minutes a day and very gradually worked up to 15 or 20 minutes.

Exercise: Daily Affirmations

Take one or two affirmations and *write them* 10 or 20 times a day. *Read them aloud* with enthusiasm. Make a song out of your affirmations and *sing them with joy.* Let your mind go over these affirmations all day long. Consistantly used affirmations become beliefs and will *always* produce results, sometimes in ways we cannot even imagine.

One of my beliefs is that I always have good relationships with my landlord. My last landlord in New York City was a man known to be extremely difficult, and all the tenants complained. In the five years I lived there, I saw him only three times. When I decided to move to California, I wanted to sell all my possessions and start fresh and unencumbered with the past. I began to do affirmations like:

"All my possessions are sold easily and quickly."

"The move is very simple to do."

"Everything is working in Divine Right Order."

"All is well."

I did not think about how difficult it would be to sell things or where I would sleep the last few nights or any other negative ideas. I just kept doing my affirmations. Well, my clients and students quickly bought all the little stuff and most of the books. I informed my landlord in a letter that I would not be renewing my lease, and to my surprise, I received a phone call from him expressing his dismay at my leaving. He offered to write me a letter of recommendation to my new landlord in California and asked if he could please buy the furniture as he had decided to rent that apartment furnished.

My Higher Consciousness had put the two beliefs together in a way I could not have conceived of, "I always have good relationships with my landlord," and "Everything will sell easily and quickly." To the other tenants' amazement, I was able to sleep in my own bed in a comfortably furnished apartment until the last moment, *AND BE PAID FOR IT!* I walked out with a few clothes, my juicer, my blender, my hair dryer, and my typewriter, plus a large check, and I leisurely took the train to Los Angeles.

Do Not Believe in Limitations

On arriving in California, it was necessary for me to buy a car. Not having owned a car before nor having made a major purchase before, I did not have any established credit. The banks would not give me credit. Being a woman and self-employed did not help my case any. I did not want to spend all my savings to buy a new car. Establishing credit became a Catch 22.

I refused to have any negative thoughts about the situation or about the banks. I rented a car and kept affirming that, "I have a beautiful new car, and it comes to me easily."

I also told everybody I met that I wanted to buy a new car and had not been able to establish credit so far. In about three months time, I met a businesswoman who instantly liked me. When I told her my story about the car, she said, "Oh well, I will take care of that."

She called a friend at the bank who owed her a favor, and told her that I was an "old" friend, and gave me the highest references. Within three days, I drove off a car dealer's lot with a beautiful new car.

I was not excited so much as I was "in awe of the process." I believe the reason it took me three months to manifest the car was that I had never committed myself to monthly payments before, and the little kid in me was scared and needed time to get up the courage to make the step.

Exercise: I Love Myself

I assume you are already saying, "I approve of myself" almost nonstop. This is a powerful basis. Keep it up for at least a month.

Now take a pad of paper and at the top write, *"I LOVE MYSELF, THEREFORE . . ."*

Finish this sentence in as many ways as you can. Read it over daily, and add to it as you think of new things.

If you can work with a partner, do so. Hold hands and alternate saying, "I love myself; therefore . . ." The biggest benefit of doing this exercise is that you learn it is almost impossible to belittle yourself when you say you love yourself.

Exercise: Claim the New

Visualize or imagine yourself having or doing or being what you are working toward. Fill in all the details. Feel,

see, taste, touch, hear. Notice other peoples' reactions to
your new state. Make it all okay with you no matter what
their reactions are.

Exercise: Expand Your Knowledge

Read everything you can to expand your awareness and
understanding of how the mind works. There is so much
knowledge out there for you. This book is only *ONE STEP*
on your pathway! Get other viewpoints. Hear other people
say it in a different way. Study with a group for a while
until you go beyond them.

This is a life work. The more you learn, the more you
know, the more you practice and apply, the better you get
to feel, and the more wonderful your life will be. Doing this
work makes *YOU FEEL GOOD!*

Begin to Demonstrate Results

By practicing as many of these methods as you can, you will
begin to demonstrate your results of this work. You will see the
little miracles occur in your life. The things you are ready to
eliminate will go of their own accord. The things and events you
want will pop up in your life seemingly out of the blue. You will
get bonuses you never imagined!

I was so surprised and delighted when after a few months of
doing my mental work, I began to look younger. Today I look ten
years younger than I did ten years ago!

Love who and what you are and what you do. Laugh at yourself and at life, and nothing can touch you. It's all temporary
anyway. Next lifetime you will do it differently anyway, so why
not do it differently right now?

You could read one of Norman Cousins' books. He cured himself of a fatal disease with laughter. Unfortunately, he didn't change
the mental patterns that created that disease, and so just created
another one. However, he also laughed himself to health on that
one, too!

There are so many ways you can approach your healing. Try

them all, and then use the ones that appeal to you the most.

When you go to bed at night, close your eyes and again be thankful for all the good in your life. It will bring more good in.

Please do not listen to the news or watch it on TV the last thing at night. The news is only a list of disasters, and you don't want to take that into your dream state. Much clearing work is done in the dream state, and you can ask your dreams for help with anything you are working on. You will often find an answer by morning.

Go to sleep peacefully. Trust the process of life to be on your side and take care of everything for your highest good and greatest joy.

There is no need to make drudgery out of what you are doing. It can be fun. It can be a game. It can be a joy. It's up to you! Even practicing forgiveness and releasing resentment can be fun, if you want to make it so. Again, make up a little song about that person or situation that is so hard to release. When you sing a ditty, it lightens up the whole procedure. When I work with clients privately, I bring laughter into the procedure as soon as I can. The quicker we can laugh about the whole thing, the easier it is to let it go.

If you saw your problems on a stage in a play by Neil Simon, you would laugh yourself right out of the chair. Tragedy and comedy are the same things. It just depends on your viewpoint! "Oh, what fools we mortals be."

Do whatever you can to make your transformational change a joy and a pleasure. Have fun!

In the infinity of life where I am, all is perfect,
whole and complete. I support myself, and life supports me.
I see evidence of The Law working all around me
and in every area of my life.
I reinforce that which I learn in joyous ways.
My day begins with gratitude and joy.
I look forward with enthusiasm to the adventures of the day,
knowing that in my life, "All is good."
I love who I am and all that I do.
I am the living, loving, joyous expression of life.
All is well in my world.

Part 3
PUTTING THESE IDEAS TO WORK

♥ Chapter Ten
RELATIONSHIPS

"All my relationships are harmonious"

It seems all of life is relationships. We have relationships with everything. You are even having a relationship now with the book you are reading and with me and my concepts.

The relationships you have with objects and foods and weather and transportation and with people all reflect the relationship you have with yourself. The relationship you have with yourself is highly influenced by the relationships you had with the adults around you as a child. The way the adults reacted to us then is often the way we react toward ourselves now, both positively and negatively.

Think for a moment of the words you use when you are scolding yourself. Aren't they the same words your parents used when they were scolding you? What words did they use when they praised you? I'm sure you use the same words to praise yourself.

Perhaps they never praised you, so then you have no idea how to praise yourself and probably think you have nothing to praise. I am not blaming our parents, because we are all victims of victims. They could not possibly teach you anything they did not know.

Sondra Ray, the great Rebirther who has done so much work with relationships, claims that every major relationship we have is a reflection of the relationship we had with one of our parents. She also claims that until we clean up that first one, we will never be free to create exactly what we want in relationships.

Relationships are mirrors of ourselves. What we attract always mirrors either qualities we have or beliefs we have about relationships. This is true whether it is a boss, a coworker, an employee, a friend, a lover, a spouse, or child. The things you don't like about these people are either what you yourself do or would like to do, or what you believe. You could not attract them or have them in your life if the way they are didn't somehow complement your own life.

Exercise: Us vs. Them

Look for a moment at someone in your life who bothers you. Describe three things about this person that you don't like, things that you want them to change.

Now look deeply inside of you and ask yourself, "Where am I like that, and when do I do the same things?"

Close your eyes and give yourself the time to do this.

Then ask yourself if you *ARE WILLING TO CHANGE.* When you remove these patterns, habits and beliefs from your thinking and behavior, either they will change or leave your life.

If you have a boss who is critical and impossible to please, look within. Either you do that on some level or you have a belief that "Bosses are always critical and impossible to please."

If you have an employee who won't obey or doesn't follow through, look to see where you do that and clean it up. Firing someone is too easy; it doesn't clear your pattern.

If there is a coworker who won't cooperate and be part of the team, look to see how you could have attracted this. Where are you noncooperative?

If you have a friend who is undependable and lets you down, turn within. Where in your life are you undependable, and when do you let others down? Is that your belief?

If you have a lover who is cold and seems unloving, look to see if there is a belief within you that came from watching your parents in your childhood that says, "Love is cold and undemonstrative."

If you have a spouse who is nagging and nonsupportive, again look to your childhood beliefs. Did you have a parent who was nagging and nonsupportive? Are you that way?

If you have a child who has habits that irritate you, I will guarantee that they are your habits. Children learn only by imitating the adults around them. Clear it within you, and you'll find that they change automatically.

This is the *only* way to change others — change ourselves first. Change your patterns, and you will find "they" are different too.

Blame is useless. Blaming only gives away our power. Keep your power. Without power, we cannot make changes. The helpless victim cannot see a way out.

Attracting Love

Love comes when we least expect it, when we are not looking for it. Hunting for love never brings the right partner. It only creates longing and unhappiness. Love is never outside ourselves; love is within us.

Don't insist that love come immediately. Perhaps you are not ready for it, or you are not developed enough to attract the love you want.

Don't settle for anybody just to have someone. Set your standards. What kind of love do you want to attract? List the qualities you really want in the relationship. Develop those qualities in yourself and you will attract a person who has them.

You might examine what may be keeping love away. Could it be criticism? Feelings of unworthiness? Unreasonable standards? Movie star images? Fear of intimacy? A belief that you are unlovable?

Be ready for love when it does come. Prepare the field and be ready to nourish love. Be loving, and you will be lovable. Be open and receptive to love.

In the infinity of life where I am,
all is perfect, whole and complete.
I live in harmony and balance with everyone I know.
Deep at the center of my being, there is an infinite well of love.
I now allow this love to flow to the surface.
It fills my heart, my body, my mind, my consciousness,
my very being, and radiates out from me in all directions
and returns to me multiplied.
The more love I use and give, the more I have to give.
The supply is endless.
The use of love makes me feel good,
it is an expression of my inner joy. I love myself;
therefore, I take loving care of my body.
I lovingly feed it nourishing foods and beverages,
I lovingly groom it and dress it, and my body lovingly
responds to me with vibrant health and energy.
I love myself; therefore, I provide for myself a comfortable home,
one that fills all my needs and is a pleasure to be in.
I fill the rooms with the vibration of love
so that all who enter, myself included, will feel this love
and be nourished by it.

*I love myself; therefore, I work at a job I truly enjoy doing,
one that uses my creative talents and abilities,
working with and for people I love and who love me,
and earning a good income.
I love myself; therefore, I behave and think in a loving way
to all people for I know that that which I give out
returns to me multiplied.
I only attract loving people in my world,
for they are a mirror of what I am.
I love myself; therefore, I forgive and totally release the past
and all past experiences and I am free.
I love myself; therefore, I live totally in the now,
experiencing each moment as good and knowing that my future
is bright and joyous and secure,
for I am a beloved child of the Universe
and the Universe lovingly takes care of me
now and forever more. All is well in my world.*

Chapter Eleven
WORK

"I am deeply fulfilled by all that I do."

Wouldn't you love to have the above affirmation be true for you? Perhaps you have been limiting yourself by thinking some of these thoughts:

I can't stand this job.

I hate my boss.

I don't earn enough money.

They don't appreciate me at work.

I can't get along with the people at work.

I don't know what I want to do.

This is negative, defensive thinking. What kind of good position do you think this will get you? It is approaching the subject from the wrong end.

If you are in a job you don't care for, if you want to change your position, if you are having problems at work, or if you are out of work, the best way to handle it is this:

Begin by blessing your current position with love. Realize that this is only a stepping stone on your pathway. You are where you are because of your own thinking patterns. If "they" are not treating you the way you would like to be treated, then there is a pattern in your consciousness that is attracting such behavior. So, in your mind, look around your current job or the job you had last and begin to bless everything with love — the building, the elevators or stairs, the rooms, the furniture and equipment, the people you work for and the people you work with — and each and every customer.

Begin to affirm for yourself that, "I always work for the most wonderful bosses," "My Boss always treats me with respect and courtesy," and, "My boss is generous and easy to work for." This will carry forward with you all your life, and if you become a boss, then you will be like that too.

A young man was about to start a new job and was nervous. I remember saying, "Why wouldn't you do well? Of *course* you will be successful. Open your heart and let your talents flow out of you. Bless the establishment, the people you work with, and the people you work for, and each and every customer with love, and all will go well."

He did just that and was a great success.

If you want to leave your job, then begin to affirm that you release' your current job with love to the next person who will be delighted to have it. Know that there are people out there looking for exactly what you have to offer, and that you are being brought together on the checkerboard of life even now.

Affirmation for Work

"I am totally open and receptive to a wonderful new position, one that uses all my talents and abilities, and allows me to express creatively in ways that are fulfilling to me. I work with and for people whom I love, and who love and respect me, in a wonderful location and earning good money."

If there is someone at work who bothers you, again bless them with love every time you think of them. In each and every one of us is every single quality. *While we may not choose to do so, we are all capable of being a Hitler or a Mother Theresa.* If this person is critical, begin to affirm that he or she is loving and full of praise. If they are grouchy, affirm that they are cheerful and fun to be around. If they are cruel, affirm that they are gentle and compassionate. If you see only the good qualities in this person, then that is what he or she has to show to you, not matter how they behave toward others.

Example

His new job was to play the piano in a club where the boss was known for being unkind and mean. The employees used to call the boss "Mr. Death" behind his back. I was asked how to handle this situation.

I replied, "Inside each and every person are all the good qualities. No matter how other people react to him, it has nothing to do with you. Every time you think of this man, bless him with love. Keep affirming for yourself, I always work for wonderful bosses. Keep doing this over and over."

He took my advice and did exactly that. My client began to receive warm greetings, and the boss soon began to slip him bonuses and hired him to play in several other clubs. The other employees who were sending out negative thoughts to the boss were still being mistreated.

If you like your job, but feel you are not getting paid enough, then begin to bless your current salary with love. Expressing gratitude for what we already have enables it to grow. Affirm that you are now opening your consciousness to a greater prosperity and that *PART* of that prosperity is an increased salary. Affirm that you deserve a raise, not for negative reasons, but because you are a great asset to the company and they want to share their profits with you. Always do the best you can on the job, for then the Universe will know that you are ready to be lifted out of where you are to the next and even better place.

Your consciousness put you where you are now. Your consciousness will either keep you there or lift you to a better position. It's up to you.

In the infinity of life where I am,
all is perfect, whole and complete.
My unique creative talents and abilities flow through me
and are expressed in deeply satisfying ways.
There are people out there who are always
looking for my services. I am always in demand
and can pick and choose what I want to do.
I earn good money doing what satisfies me.
My work is a joy and a pleasure.
All is well in my world.

 *Chapter Twelve*
SUCCESS

"Every Experience is a Success."

What does "failure" mean anyway? Does it mean that something did not turn out the way you wanted it to, or the way you were hoping? The law of experience is always perfect. We outpicture our inner thoughts and beliefs perfectly. You must have left out a step or had an inner belief that told you you did not deserve — or you felt unworthy.

It's the same when I work with my computer. If there's a mistake, it is always me. It is something I have not done to comply with the laws of the computer. It only means that there is something else for me to learn.

The old saying, "If at first you don't succeed, try, try again," is *so* true. It doesn't mean beat yourself up and try the same old way again. It means recognize your error and try another way — until you learn to do it correctly.

I think it is our natural birthright to go from success to success all our life. If we are not doing that, either we are not in tune with our innate capabilities, or we do not believe it can be true for us, or we do not recognize our successes.

When we set standards that are much too high for where we are at this moment, standards we cannot possibly achieve right now, then we will always fail.

When a little child is learning to walk or talk, we encourage it and praise it for every tiny improvement the child makes. The child beams and eagerly tries to do better. Is this the way you encourage yourself when you are learning something new? Or do you make it harder to learn because you tell yourself that you are stupid or clumsy or a "failure."

Many actresses and actors feel they must be performance perfect when they arrive at the first rehearsal. I remind them that the purpose of rehearsal is to learn. Rehearsal is a period of time to make mistakes, to try new ways and to learn. Only by practicing over and over do we learn the new and make it a natural part of us. When you watch an accomplished professional in any field, you are looking at innumerable hours of practice.

Don't do what I used to do — I would refuse to try anything new because I didn't know how to do it and I didn't want to appear foolish. Learning is making mistakes until our subconscious mind can put together the right pictures.

It doesn't matter how long you have been thinking of yourself as a failure; you can begin to create a "success" pattern now. It doesn't matter what field you want to operate in. The principles are the same. We need to plant the "seeds" of success. These seeds will grow into an abundant harvest.

Here are some "success" affirmations you can use:

Divine Intelligence gives me all the ideas I can use.

Everything I touch is a success.

There is plenty for everyone, including me.

There are plenty of customers for my services.

I establish a new awareness of success.

I move into the Winning Circle.

I am a magnet for Divine Prosperity.

I am blessed beyond my fondest dreams.

Riches of every sort are drawn to me.

Golden Opportunities are everywhere for me.

Pick one of the above affirmations and repeat it for several days. Then pick another and do the same. Allow these ideas to fill your consciousness. Don't worry about "how" to accomplish this; the opportunities will come your way. Trust the intelligence within you to lead you and guide you. You deserve to be a success in every area of your life.

In the infinity of life where I am,
all is perfect, whole and complete.
I am one with the Power that created me.
I have within me all the ingredients for success.
I now allow the success formula to flow through me
and manifest in my world.
Whatever I am guided to do will be a success.
I learn from every experience.
I go from success to success and from glory to glory.
My pathway is a series of stepping stones
to ever greater successes.
All is well in my world.

Chapter Thirteen
PROSPERITY

"I deserve the best, and I accept the best, now."

If you want the above affirmation to be true for you, then you do not want to believe any of the following statements:

Money doesn't grow on trees.
Money is filthy and dirty.
Money is evil.
I am poor, but clean, or good.
Rich people are crooks.
I don't want to have money and be stuck up.
I will never get a good job.
I will never make any money.
Money goes out faster than it comes in.
I am always in debt.
Poor people can never get out from under.
My parents were poor and I will be poor.
Artists have to struggle.
Only people who cheat have money.
Everyone else comes first.
Oh I couldn't charge that much.
I don't deserve.
I'm not good enough to make money.
Never tell anyone what I have in the bank.
Don't lend money.

A penny saved is a penny earned.

Save for a rainy day.

A depression could come at any moment.

I resent others having money.

Money only comes from hard work.

How many of these beliefs belong to you? Do you really think that believing any of them will bring you prosperity?

It is old limited thinking. Perhaps it was what your family believed about money because family beliefs stay with us unless we consciously release them. Wherever it came from, it must leave your consciousness if you want to prosper.

To me, true prosperity begins with feeling good about yourself. It is also the freedom to do what you want to do, when you want to do it. It is never an amount of money, it is a state of mind. Prosperity or lack of it is an outer expression of the ideas in your head.

Deserving

If we do not accept the idea that we "deserve" to prosper, then even when abundance falls in our laps, we will refuse it somehow. Look at this example:

A student in one of my classes was working to increase his prosperity. He came to class one night *so* excited, for he had just won $500. He kept saying, "I don't believe it! I never win anything." We knew it was a reflection of his changing consciousness. He still felt he did not really deserve it. Next week he could not come to class as he had broken his leg. The doctor bills came to $500.

He had been frightened to "move forward" in a new "prosperous direction" and felt undeserving, so he punished himself in this way.

Whatever we concentrate on increases, so don't concentrate on your bills. If you concentrate on lack and debt, then you will create more lack and debt.

There is an inexhaustible supply in the Universe. Begin to be aware of it. Take the time to count the stars on a clear evening, or the grains of sand in one handful, the leaves on one branch of a tree, the raindrops on a windowpane, the seeds in one tomato. Each seed is capable of producing a whole vine with unlimited tomatoes on it. Be grateful for what you do have and you will find it increases. I like to bless with love all that is in my life now, my home, the heat, water, light, telephone, furniture, plumbing, appliances, clothing, transportation, jobs — the money I do have, friends, my ability to see and feel and taste and touch and walk and to enjoy this incredible planet.

Our own belief in lack and limitation is the only thing that is limiting us. What belief is limiting you?

Do you want to have money only to help others? Then you are saying you are worthless.

Be sure you are not rejecting prosperity now. If a friend invites you to lunch or dinner, accept with joy and pleasure. Don't feel you are just "trading" with people. If you get a gift, accept it graciously. If you can't use the gift, pass it on to someone else. Keep the flow of things moving through you. Just smile and say "Thank you." This way you let the Universe know you are ready to receive your good.

Make Room for the New

Make room for the new. Clean out your refrigerator, get rid of all those little bits of stuff wrapped in foil. Clean out your closets, get rid of all the stuff you have not used in the last six months or so. If you haven't used it in a year, definitely get it out of your home. Sell it, trade it, give it away, or burn it.

Cluttered closets mean a cluttered mind. As you clean the closet, say to yourself, "I am cleaning out the closets of my mind." The Universe loves symbolic gestures.

The first time I heard the concept, "The abundance of the Universe is available to everyone," I thought it was ridiculous.

"Look at all the poor people," I said to myself. "Look at my own seemingly hopeless poverty." To hear, "Your poverty is only a belief in your consciousness" only made me angry. It took me

many years to realize and accept that I was the only person responsible for my lack of prosperity. It was my belief I was "unworthy," and "not deserving," that "Money is difficult to come
by," and that "I do not have talents and abilities," that kept me
stuck in a mental system of "not having."

MONEY IS THE EASIEST THING TO DEMONSTRATE!
How do you react to this statement? Do you believe it? Are you
angry? Are you indifferent? Are you ready to throw this book
across the room? If you have any of these reactions, *GOOD!* I
have touched something deep inside you, that very point of resistance to truth. This is the area to work on. It is time to open yourself to the potential of receiving the flow of money and all good.

Love Your Bills

It is essential that we stop worrying about money and stop
resenting our bills. Many people treat bills as punishments to be
avoided if possible. A bill is an acknowledgement of our ability to
pay. The creditor assumes you are affluent enough and gives you
the service or the product first. I bless with love each and every
bill that comes into my home. I bless with love and stamp a small
kiss on each and every check I write. If you pay with resentment,
money has a hard time coming back to you. If you pay with love
and joy, you open the freeflowing channel of abundance. Treat
your money as a friend, not as something you wad up and crush
into your pocket.

Your security is not your job, or your bank account, nor your
investments, nor your spouse or parents. Your security is your
ability to connect with the cosmic power that creates all things.

I like to think that the power within me that breathes in my body
is the same power that provides all that I need, and just as easily
and simply. The Universe is lavish and abundant and it is our
birthright to be supplied with everything we need, unless we
choose to believe it to the contrary.

I bless my telephone with love each time I use it, and I affirm often that it brings me only prosperity and expressions of love. I do the same with my mail box, and each day it is filled to overflowing with money and love letters of all kinds from friends and clients and far off readers of my book. The bills that come in I rejoice over, thanking the companies for trusting me to pay. I bless my doorbell and the front door, knowing that only good comes into my home. I expect my life to be good and joyous, and it is.

These Ideas are for Everyone

He was a hooker and wanted to increase his business, so he came to me for a prosperity session. He felt he was good at his profession and wanted to make $100,000 a year. I gave him the same ideas I am giving you, and soon he had money to put into Chinese porcelains. He spent so much time at home, he wanted to enjoy the beauty of his ever increasing investments.

Rejoice in Others' Good Fortune

Don't delay your own prosperity by being resentful or jealous that someone else has more than you. Don't criticize the way they choose to spend their money. It is none of your business.

Each person is under the law of his or her own consciousness. Just take care of your own thoughts. Bless another's good fortune, and know there is plenty for all.

Are you a stingy tipper? Do you stiff washroom attendants with some self-righteous statement? Do you ignore the porters in your office or apartment building at Christmas time? Do you pinch pennies when you don't need to buying day-old vegetables or bread? Do you do your shopping in a thrift shop, or do you always order the cheapest thing on the menu?

There is a law of "demand and supply." Demand comes first. Money has a way of coming to where it is needed. The poorest family can almost always gather together the money for a funeral.

Visualization – Ocean of Abundance

Your prosperity consciousness is not dependent on money; your flow of money is dependent upon your prosperity consciousness.

As you can conceive of more, more will come into your life.

I love the visualization of standing at the sea shore looking out at the vast ocean and knowing that this ocean is the abundance that is available to me. Look down at your hands and see what sort of container you are holding. Is it a teaspoon, a thimble with a hole in it, a paper cup, a glass, a tumbler, a pitcher, a bucket, a wash tub, or perhaps you have a pipeline connected to this ocean of abundance? Look around you and notice that no matter how many people there are and no matter what kind of container they have, there is plenty for everyone. You cannot rob another, and they cannot rob you. And in no way can you drain the ocean dry. Your container is your consciousness, and it can always be exchanged for a larger container. Do this exercise often, to get the feeling of expansion and unlimited supply.

Open Your Arms

I sit at least once a day with my arms stretched out to the side and say, "I am open and receptive to all the good and abundance in the Universe." It gives me a feeling of expansion.

The Universe can only distribute to me what I have in my consciousness, and I can *ALWAYS* create more in my consciousness. It is like a cosmic bank. I make mental deposits by increasing my awareness of my own abilities to create. Meditation, treatments, and affirmations are mental deposits. Let's make a habit of making daily deposits.

Just having more money is not enough. We want to enjoy the money. Do you allow yourself to have pleasure with money? If not, why not? A portion of everything you take in can go to pure pleasure. Did you have any fun with your money last week? Why not? What old belief is stopping you? Let it go.

Money does not have to be a serious subject in your life. Put it into perspective. Money is a means of exchange. That's all it is. What would you do and what would you have if you didn't need money?

Jerry Gilles, who has written *MONEY LOVE,* one of the best books I know on money, suggests we create a "poverty penalty" for ourselves. Every time we think or say a negative about our money situation, we fine ourselves a certain amount and put it in a container. At the end of the week, we have to spend this money on pleasure.

We need to shake up our money concepts. I have found it is easier to teach a seminar on sexuality than it is one on money. People get very angry when their money beliefs are being challenged. Even people who come to a seminar wanting desperately to create more money in their lives will go crazy when I try to change their limiting beliefs.

"I am willing to change." "I am willing to release old negative beliefs." Sometimes we have to work with these two affirmations a lot in order to open the space to begin creating prosperity.

We want to release the "fixed income" mentality. Do not limit the Universe by insisting that you have *"ONLY"* a certain salary or income. That salary or income is a *CHANNEL; IT IS NOT YOUR SOURCE.* Your supply comes from one source, the Universe itself.

There are an infinite number of channels. We must open ourselves to them. We must accept in consciousness that supply can come from anywhere and everywhere. Then when we walk down the street and find a penny or a dime, we say "Thank You!" to the source. It may be small, but new channels are beginning to open.

"I am open and receptive to new avenues of income."

"I now receive my good from expected and unexpected sources."

"I am an unlimited being accepting from an unlimited source in an unlimited way."

Rejoice in the Small New Beginnings

When we work for increasing prosperity, we always gain in accordance with our beliefs about what we deserve. A writer was working to increase her income. One of her affirmations was, "I am making good money being a writer." Three days later, she went to a coffee shop where she often had breakfast. She settled into a booth and spread out some papers she was working on. The manager came over to her and asked, "You are a writer, aren't you? Will you do some writing for me?"

He then brought over several little blank tent signs and asked if she would write, *"TURKEY LUNCHEON SPECIAL, $3.95,"* on each card. He offered her a free breakfast in return.

This small event showed the beginning of her change in consciousness and she went on to selling her works.

Recognize Prosperity

Begin to recognize prosperity everywhere and rejoice in it. Reverend Ike, the well-known evangelist in New York City, remembers as a poor preacher he used to walk by good restaurants and homes and automobiles and clothing establishments and say out loud, "That's for me, that's for me." Allow fancy homes and banks and fine stores and showrooms of all sorts — and yachts — to give you pleasure. Recognize that all this is part of *YOUR* abundance, and you are increasing your consciousness to partake of these things if you desire. If you see well-dressed people, think, "Isn't it wonderful that they have so much abundance? There is plenty for all of us."

We don't want someone else's good. We want to have our *own* good.

And yet we do not own anything. We only use possessions for a period of time until they pass on to someone else. Sometimes a possession may stay in a family for a few generations, but eventually it will pass on. There is a natural rhythm and flow of life. Things come, and things go. I believe that when something goes, it is only to make room for something new and better.

Accept Compliments

So many people want to be rich, and yet they won't accept a compliment. I have many a budding actor and actress who want to be a "star," and yet he or she cringes at a compliment.

Compliments are gifts of prosperity. Learn to accept them graciously. My mother taught me early to smile and say, "Thank you" when I received a compliment or a gift. It has been an asset all my life.

It is even better to accept the compliment and return it so the giver feels as though he or she has received a gift. It is a way of keeping the flow of good going.

Rejoice in the abundance of being able to awaken each morning and experience a new day. Be glad to be alive, to be healthy, to have friends, to be creative, to be a living example of the joy of living. Live to your highest awareness. Enjoy your transformational process.

In the infinity of life where I am,
all is perfect, whole and complete.
I am one with the Power that created me.
I am totally open and receptive to the abundant flow of
prosperity that the Universe offers.
All my needs and desires are met before I even ask.
I am Divinely guided and protected,
and I make choices that are beneficial for me.
I rejoice in other's successes, knowing there is plenty for us all.
I am constantly increasing my conscious awareness of abundance,
and this reflects in a constantly increasing income.
My good comes from everywhere and everyone.
All is well in my world.

♥ Chapter Fourteen
THE BODY

"I listen with love to my body's messages."

I believe we create every so called "illness" in our body. The body, like everything else in life, is a mirror of our inner thoughts and beliefs. The body is always talking to us, if we will only take the time to listen. Every cell within your body responds to every single thought you think and every word you speak.

Continuous modes of thinking and speaking produce body behaviors and postures and eases or dis-eases. The person who has a permanently scowling face did not produce that by having joyous, loving thoughts. Older people's faces and bodies show so clearly a lifetime of thinking patterns. How will you look when you are elderly?

I am including in this section my list of Probable Mental Patterns that create illnesses in the body, as well as the New Thought Patterns or Affirmations to be used to create health. They appear in my book *HEAL YOUR BODY*. In addition to those short listings, I will explore a few of the more common conditions to give you an idea of just how we create these problems.

Not every mental equivalent is 100 percent true for everyone. However, it does give us a point of reference to begin our search for the cause of the disease. Many people working in the alternative healing therapies use *HEAL YOUR BODY* all the time with their clients and find that the mental causes run 90 or 95 percent true.

* * *

THE HEAD represents us. It is what we show the world. It is how we are usually recognized. When something is wrong in the head area, it usually means we feel something is very wrong with "us."

THE HAIR represents strength. When we are tense and afraid, we often create those bands of steel that originate in the shoulder muscles and come up over the top of the head and sometimes even down around the eyes. The hair shaft grows up through the hair follicle. When there is a lot of tension in the scalp, the hair shaft can be squeezed so tightly that the hair can no longer breathe, and it dies and falls out. If this tension is continued, and the scalp is not relaxed, then the follicle remains so tight that the new hair cannot grow through. The result is baldness.

Female baldness has been on the increase ever since women have begun entering the "business world" with all its tensions and frustrations. We are not so aware of baldness in women because women's wigs are so natural and attractive. Unfortunately, most men's toupees are still discernible at quite a distance.

Tension is not being strong. Tension is weakness. Being relaxed and centered and peaceful is really being strong and secure. It would be good for us to relax our bodies more, and many of us need to relax our scalps too.

Try it now. Tell your scalp to relax and feel if there is a difference. If you notice that your scalp visibly relaxes, then I would suggest you do this little exercise often.

THE EARS represent the capacity to hear. When there are problems with the ears, it usually means something is going on you do not want to hear. An earache would indicate that there is anger about what is heard.

Earaches are common with children. They often have to listen to stuff going on in the household they really don't want to hear. Household rules often forbid a child's expression of anger, and the child's inability to change things creates an earache.

Deafness represents longstanding refusal to listen to someone. Notice that when one partner has a hearing impairment, the other partner often talks and talks and talks.

THE EYES represent the capacity to see. When there are problems with the eyes, it usually means there is something we do not want to see, either about ourselves or about life; past, present or future.

Whenever I see small children wearing glasses, I know there is stuff going on in their household they do not want to look at. If they can't change the experience, they will diffuse the sight so they don't have to see it so clearly.

Many people have had dramatic healing experiences when they have been willing to go back into the past and clean up what it was they did not want to look at a year or two before they began wearing glasses.

Are you negating what's happening right now? What don't you want to face? Are you afraid to see the present or the future? If you could see clearly, what would you see that you don't see now? Can you see what you are doing to yourself?

Interesting questions to look at.

HEADACHES come from invalidating the self. The next time you get a headache, stop and ask yourself where and how you have just made yourself wrong. Forgive yourself, let it go, and the headache will dissolve back into the nothingness from whence it came.

Migraine headaches are created by people who want to be perfect and who create a lot of pressure on themselves. A lot of suppressed anger is involved. Interestingly, migraine headaches can almost always be alleviated by masturbation if you do it as soon as you feel a migraine coming on. The sexual release dissolves the tension and the pain. You may not feel like masturbating then, but it certainly is worth a try. You can't lose.

SINUS problems, felt right in the face and so close to the nose, represent being irritated by someone in your life, someone who is close to you. You might even feel they are bearing down on you.

We forget that we create the situations, then we give our power away by blaming the other person for our frustration. No person, no place, and no thing has any power over us, for "we" are the only thinkers in our mind. We create our experiences, our reality,

and everyone in it. When we create peace and harmony and balance in our mind, we will find it in our lives.

THE NECK AND THROAT are fascinating because so much
"stuff" goes on there. The neck represents the ability to be flexible
in our thinking, to see the other side of a question, and to see
another person's viewpoint. When there are problems with the
neck, it usually means we are being stubborn about our own concept of a situation.

Whenever I see a person wearing one of those "collars," I know
this person is being very self-righteous and stubborn about not
seeing the other side of an issue.

Virginia Satir, the brilliant family therapist, says she did some
"silly research" and found that there are more than 250 different
ways to wash dishes, depending upon who is washing and the ingredients used. If we are stuck in believing there is only "one way,"
or "one viewpoint," then we are shutting out most of life.

THE THROAT represents our ability to "speak up" for ourselves, to "ask for what we want," to say "I am," etc. When we
have throat problems, it usually means we do not feel we have the
right to do these things. We feel inadequate to stand up for ourselves.

Sore throats are always anger. If a cold is involved, then there is
mental confusion too. LARYNGITIS usually means you are so
angry you cannot speak.

The throat also represents the creative flow in the body. This is
where we express our creativity; and when our creativity is stifled
and frustrated, we often have throat problems. We all know many
people who live their whole lives for others. They never once get
to do what they want to do. They are always pleasing mothers/
fathers/spouses/lovers/bosses. TONSILLITIS and THYROID
problems are just frustrated creativity not being able to do what
you want to do.

The energy center in the throat, the fifth chakra, is the place in
the body where change takes place. When we are resisting change
or are in the middle of change or are trying to change, we often
have a lot of activity in our throats. Notice when you cough, or

when someone else coughs. What has just been said? What are we reacting to? Is it resistance and stubbornness, or is it the process of change taking place? In a workshop I use coughs as a tool for self-discovery. Every time someone coughs, I have that person touch the throat and say out loud, "I am willing to change," or "I am changing."

THE ARMS represent our ability and capacity to embrace the experiences of life. The upper arms have to do with our capacity, and the lower arms have to do with our abilities. We store old emotions in our joints, and the elbows represent our flexibility in changing directions. Are you flexible about a changing direction in your life, or are old emotions keeping you stuck in one spot?

THE HANDS grasp, hands hold, hands clench. We let things slip through our fingers. Sometimes we hold on too long. We are handy, tightfisted, openhanded, penny pinchers, butterfingers. We give handouts. We can handle ourselves, or we can't seem to handle anything.

We put a handle on something. It's hands down. It's hands off, hanky panky. We give someone a hand, are hand in hand, it's on hand or out of hand, underhanded or overhanded. We have helping hands.

Hands can be gentle, or they can be hard with knotty knuckles from overthinking or gnarled with arthritic criticism. Grasping hands come from fear; fear of loss, fear of never having enough, fear that it won't stay if you hold lightly.

Tightly grasping a relationship only has the partner run away in desperation. Tightly clenched hands cannot take in anything new. Shaking the hands freely from the wrists gives a feeling of looseness and openness.

That which belongs to you cannot be taken from you, so relax.

THE FINGERS each have meaning. Problems in the fingers show where you need to relax and let go. If you cut your index finger, there is probably anger and fear that has to do with your ego in some current situation. The thumb is mental and represents worry. The index finger is the ego and fear. The middle finger has to do with sex and with anger. When angry hold your middle finger and watch the anger dissolve. Hold the right finger if your anger is at a man and the left if it is at a woman. The ring finger is both unions and grief. The little finger has to do with the family and pretending.

THE BACK represents our support system. Problems with the back usually mean we feel we are not being supported. Too often we think we are only supported by our job or by our family or spouses. In reality, we are totally supported by the Universe, by Life itself.

The upper back has to do with feeling the lack of emotional support. My husband/wife/lover/friend/boss doesn't understand me or support me.

The middle back has to do with guilt. All that stuff that is in back of us. Are you afraid to see what is back there, or are you hiding what is back there? Do you feel stabbed in the back?

Do you feel real "burnt out"? Are your finances in a mess, or do you worry about them excessively? Then your lower back may be bothering you. The lack of money or the fear of money will do it. The amount you have has nothing to do with it.

So many of us feel that money is the most important thing in our lives, and that we could not live without it. This is not true. There is something far more important and precious to us without which we could not live. What is that? It is our breath.

Our breath is the most precious substance in our lives, and yet we totally take for granted when we exhale that our next breath will be there. If we did not take another breath, we would not last three minutes. Now if the Power that created us has given us enough breath to last for as long as we shall live, can we not trust that everything else we need will also be supplied?

THE LUNGS represent our capacity to take in and give out life. Problems with the lungs usually mean we are afraid to take in life, or perhaps we feel we do not have the right to live fully.

Women have traditionally been very shallow breathers and have often thought of themselves as second class citizens who did not have the right to take up space and sometimes not even the right to live. Today this is all changing. Women are taking their place as full members of society and breathing deeply and fully.

It pleases me to see women in sports. Women have always worked in the fields; but this is the first time in history, as far as I know, that women have gone into sports. It is wonderful to see the magnificent bodies that are emerging.

Emphysema and heavy smoking are ways of denying life. They mask a deep feeling of being totally unworthy of existing. Scolding will not change the habit of smoking. It is the basic belief that must change first.

THE BREASTS represent the mothering principle. When there are problems with the breasts, it usually means we are "over-mothering" either a person, a place, a thing, or an experience.

Part of the mothering process is to allow the child to "grow up." We need to know when to take our hands off, when to turn over the reins and let them be. Being overprotective does not prepare the other person to handle his or her own experience. Sometimes our "overbearing" attitudes literally cut off nourishment in a situation.

If cancer is involved, then there is also deep resentment. Release the fear and know the Intelligence of the Universe resides in each one of us.

THE HEART, of course, represents love, while our blood represents joy. Our hearts lovingly pump joy throughout our bodies. When we deny ourselves joy and love, the heart shrivels and becomes cold. As a result, the blood gets sluggish and we creep our way to ANEMIA, ANGINA, and HEART ATTACKS.

The heart does not "attack" us. We get so caught up in the soap opera and dramas we create that we often forget to notice the little joys that surround us. We spend years squeezing all the joy out of the heart, and it literally falls over in pain. Heart attack people are never joyous people. If they do not take the time to appreciate the joys of life, they will just recreate another heart attack in time.

Heart of gold, cold heart, open heart, black heart, loving heart, warm hearted — where is your heart?

THE STOMACH digests all the new ideas and experiences we

have. What or who can't you stomach? What gets you in the gut?

When there are stomach problems, it usually means we don't know how to assimilate the new experience. We are afraid.

Many of us remember when commercial airplanes first became popular. That we could get inside a big metal tube that would carry us safely through the sky was a new idea we found hard to assimilate.

At every seat there were throw up bags, and most of us were using them. We would throw up into our barf bags as discreetly as we could, wrap them up and hand them to the stewardess, who spent a lot of her time running up and down the aisle collecting them.

Now it is many years later, and though the bags are still at every seat, they are seldom used. We have assimilated the idea of flying.

ULCERS are no more than fear; tremendous fear of "not being good enough." We fear not being good enough for a parent, fear not being good enough for a boss. We can't stomach who we are. We rip our guts apart trying to please others. No matter how important our job is, our inner self-esteem is very low. We are afraid they will find out about us.

Love is the answer here. People who love and approve of themselves never have ulcers. Be gentle and loving to the child within, and give it all the support and encouragement you wanted when you were little.

THE GENITALS represent the most feminine part of a woman, her femininity, or the most masculine part of a man, his masculinity; our masculine principle or our feminine principle.

When we do not feel comfortable with being either a man or a woman, when we reject our sexuality, when we reject our bodies as dirty or sinful, then we often have problems in the genital area.

I seldom come across a person who was reared in a household where the genitals and their functions were called by their right names. We all grew up with euphemisms of one sort or another. Remember the ones your own family used? It could have been as mild as "down there," to names that made you feel your genitals were dirty and disgusting. Yes, we all grew up believing that something was not quite right between our legs.

I feel the sexual revolution that exploded a few years ago was in one way a good thing. We were moving away from Victorian hypocrisy. Suddenly it was okay to have many partners, and women as well as men could have one-night stands. Marital swapping became more open. Many of us began to enjoy the pleasure and freedom of our bodies in a new and open way.

However, few of us thought to deal with what Roza Lamont, founder of the Self Communication Institute, calls "Mama's God." Whatever your mother taught you about God when you were three years old is still there is your subconscious mind UNLESS you have done some conscious work to release it. Was that God an angry, avenging God? What did that God feel about sex? If we are still carrying those early guilt feelings about our sexuality and our bodies, then we are surely going to create punishment for ourselves.

BLADDER problems, ANAL problems, VAGINITIS, and PROSTATE and PENIS problems all come under the same area. They stem from distorted beliefs about our bodies and the correctness of their functions.

Every organ in our body is a magnificent expression of life with its own special functions. We do not think of our livers or our eyes as dirty or sinful. Why do we then choose to believe our genitals are?

The anus is as beautiful as the ear. Without our anus we would have no way to release what the body no longer needs, and we would die very quickly. Every part of our body and every function of our body is perfect and normal, natural and beautiful.

I ask clients with sexual problems to begin to relate to their rectum, penis, or vagina with a sense of love and appreciation for their functions and their beauty. If you are beginning to cringe or get irate as you read this, ask yourself why? Who told you to deny any part of your body? Certainly not God. Our sexual organs were created as the most pleasurable part of our body to give us pleasure. To deny this is to create pain and punishment. Sex is not only okay, it is glorious and wonderful. It is as normal for us to have sex as it is for us to breathe or eat.

Just for a moment try to visualize the vastness of the Universe. It is beyond our comprehension. Even our top scientists with their latest equipment cannot measure its size. Within this Universe there are many galaxies.

In one of these smaller galaxies in a far-off corner, there is a minor sun. Around this sun revolve a few pinpoints, one of which is called Planet Earth.

I find it hard to believe that the vast, incredible Intelligence that created this entire Universe is only an old man sitting on a cloud above the Planet Earth . . . watching my genitals!

Yet so many of us were taught this concept as a child.

It is vital that we release foolish, outmoded ideas that do not support us and nourish us. I feel strongly that even our concept of God needs to be one that is *for us,* not against us. There are so many different religions to choose from. If you have one now that tells you you are a sinner and a lowly worm, get another one.

I am not advocating that everybody run around having free sex at all times. I am saying that some of our rules do not make sense, and this is why so many people break them and become hypocrites.

When we remove sexual guilt from people and teach them to love and respect themselves, then they will automatically treat themselves and others in ways that are for their highest good and greatest joy. The reason we have so many problems with our sexuality now is because so many of us have self-hatred and self-disgust, and so we treat ourselves and others badly.

It is not enough to teach children in school the mechanics of sexuality. We need on a very deep level to allow children to remember that their bodies, genitals, and sexuality are something to rejoice about. I truly believe people who love themselves and their bodies will not abuse themselves or others.

I find that most BLADDER problems come from being "pissed off," usually at a partner. Something makes us angry that has to do with our femininity or our masculinity. Women have more bladder problems than men because they are more prone to hide their hurt. VAGINITIS again usually involves feeling romantically hurt by a partner. Men's PROSTATE problems have a lot to do with self-worth and also believing that as he gets older he becomes less of a man. IMPOTENCE adds fear and sometimes is even related to spite against a previous mate. FRIGIDITY comes from fear or a belief that it is wrong to enjoy the body. It also comes from self-disgust, and it can be intensified by an insensitive partner.

P.M.S., PRE-MENSTRUAL SYNDROME, which has reached epidemic proportions, is concurrent with the increase of media advertising. These ads continuously hammer home the concept that the female body must be sprayed and powdered and douched and over cleansed in numerous ways to make it even barely acceptable. At the same time women are coming into their own as equal beings, they are also being bombarded negatively with the idea that the feminine processes are not quite acceptable. This combined with the tremendous amounts of sugar being consumed today creates a fertile breeding ground for P.M.S.

The feminine processes, all of them, including menstruation and menopause, are normal, natural processes. We must accept them as that. Our bodies are beautiful, magnificent and wonderous.

It is my belief that VENEREAL DISEASE is almost always sexual guilt. It comes from a feeling, often subconscious, that it is not right to express ourselves sexually. A carrier with a venereal disease can have many partners, but only those whose mental and physical immune systems are weak will be susceptible to it. In addition to the old standards, in recent years the heterosexual population has created an increase of HERPES. This is a disease that comes back again and again "to punish us" for our belief that "we are bad." Herpes has a tendency to flare up when we are emotionally upset. That tells us a lot right there.

Now let's take that same theory over into the gay community, where they have all the same problems everybody else has, plus much of society pointing their fingers at them and saying, "Bad"! Usually, their own mothers and fathers are also saying, "You're bad." This is a heavy load to carry and it's difficult to love yourself under these circumstances. It is not surprising that gay men were amongst the first to experience the dread disease, AIDS.

In heterosexual society, many women dread growing old because of the belief systems we have created around the glory of youth. It is not so difficult for the men, for they become distinguished with a bit of grey hair. The older man often gets respect, and people may even look up to him.

Not so for most gay men, for they have created a culture that places tremendous emphasis on youth and beauty. While everyone is young to start with, only a few fit the standard of beauty. So much emphasis has been placed on the physical appearance of the body that the feelings inside have been totally disregarded. If you are not young and beautiful, it's almost as though you don't count. The person does not count; only the body counts.

This way of thinking is a disgrace to the whole culture. It's another way of saying "gay is not good enough."

Because of the ways gay people often treat other gays, for many gay men the experience of getting old is something to dread. It is almost better to die than to get old. And AIDS is a disease that often kills.

Too often gay men feel that when they get older, they will be useless and unwanted. It is almost better to destroy themselves first; and many have created a destructive lifestyle. Some of the concepts and attitudes that are so a part of the gay lifestyle — the meat rack, the constant judging, the refusal to get close to another, etc. — are monstrous. And AIDS is a monstrous disease.

These sorts of attitudes and behavior patterns can only create guilt on a very deep level, no matter how much we may "camp." Camping, which can be such fun, can also be extremely destructive both to givers and the recipients. It is another way of avoiding closeness and intimacy.

In no way am I trying to create guilt for anyone. However, we need to look at the things that need to be changed in order for all of our lives to function with love and joy and respect. Fifty years ago, almost all gay men were closeted, and now they have been able to create pockets in society where they can at least be relatively open. I feel it is unfortunate that much of what they have created gives so much pain to their gay brothers. While it is often deplorable the way straights treat gays, it is *tragic* the way many gays treat other gays.

Men traditionally have always had more sexual partners than women; and when men get together, of course there will be a great deal more sex. That's all fine and good. The bath houses fulfill a wonderful need, unless we are using our sexuality for the wrong reasons. Some men like having lots of partners to satisfy their deep need for self-esteem rather than for the joy of it. I do not believe there is anything wrong with having several partners, and the use of alcohol and some recreational drugs on an "occasional basis" is fine. However, if we are getting bombed out of our heads every night, and if we "need" several partners a day just to prove our self-worth, then we are not coming from a nourishing space. We need to make some mental changes.

This is a time for healing, for making whole, not for condemnation. We must rise out of the limitations of the past. We are all Divine, Magnificent expressions of Life. Let's claim that now!

THE COLON represents our ability to let go, to release that which we no longer need. The body, being in the perfect rhythm and flow of life, needs a balance of intake, assimilation, and elimination. It is only our fears that block the releasing of the old.

Even if constipated people are not actually stingy, they usually do not trust that there will ever be enough. They hold onto old relationships that give them pain. They are afraid to throw out clothes that have been in the closet for years because they might need them some day. They stay in a stifling job, or never give themselves pleasure, because they must save for that rainy day. We do not rummage in last night's garbage to find today's meal. Learn to trust the process of life always to bring you what you need.

Our LEGS carry us forward in life. Leg problems often indicate a fear of moving forward or a reluctance to move forward in a certain direction. We run with our legs, we drag our legs, we pussyfoot, we are knock-kneed, pigeon-toed; and we have big, fat, angry thighs filled with childhood resentments. Not wanting to do things will often produce minor leg problems. VARICOSE VEINS represent standing in a job or place that we hate. The veins lose their ability to carry joy.

Are *you* going in the direction you want to?

KNEES, like the neck, have to do with flexibility; only they express bending and pride, ego and stubbornness. Often when moving forward, we are fearful of bending; and we become inflexible. This stiffens the joints. We want to move forward, but we do not want to change our ways. This is why knees take so long to heal; our ego is involved. The ankle is also a joint; yet, if hurt, it can heal quite quickly. The knees take a long time because we get our pride and our self-righteousness involved.

The next time you have a knee problem, ask yourself where you are being self-righteous, where you are refusing to bend. Drop the stubbornness and let go. Life is flow, life is movement; and to be comfortable, we must be flexible and move with it. A willow tree bends and sways and flows with the wind and is always graceful and at ease with life.

Our FEET have to do with our understanding, our understanding of ourselves and of life — past, present and future.

Many old people have a difficult time walking. Their understanding has been warped, and they often feel there is no place to go. Little children move on happy, dancing feet. Elderly people often shuffle as if they are reluctant to move.

Our SKIN represents our individuality. Skin problems usually mean we feel our individuality is being threatened somehow. We feel that others have power over us. We are thin-skinned. Things get under our skin, we feel skinned alive, our nerves are right under our skin.

One of the quickest ways to heal skin problems is to nurture yourself by saying in your mind, "I approve of myself," several hundred times a day. Take back your own power.

ACCIDENTS are no accident. Like everything else in our lives, we create them. It's not that we necessarily say, "I want to have an accident," but we do have the mental thought patterns that can attract an accident to us. Some people seem to be "accident prone," and others go for a lifetime without ever getting a scratch.

Accidents are expressions of anger. They indicate built-up frustrations at not feeling the freedom to speak up for one's self. Accidents also indicate rebellion against authority. We get so mad we want to hit people, and instead, *we* get hit.

When we are angry at ourselves, when we feel guilty, when we feel the need for punishment, an accident is a marvelous way of taking care of that.

It seems as though any accident is not our fault, that we are helpless victims of a quirk of fate. An accident allows us to turn to others for sympathy and attention. We get our wounds bathed and attended too. We often get bed rest, sometimes for an extended period of time. And we get pain.

Where this pain occurs in the body gives us a clue to which area of life we feel guilty about. The degree of physical damage lets us know how severely we felt we needed to be punished and how long the sentence should be.

ANOREXIA-BULIMIA is denying the self life, an extreme form of self-hatred.

Food is nourishment on the most basic level. Why would you deny yourself nourishment? Why do you want to die? What is going on in your life that is so awful that you want to get out completely?

Self-hatred is only hating a thought you have about yourself. Thoughts can be changed.

What is so terrible about you? Were you reared in a critical family? Did you have critical teachers? Did your early religious training tell you you were "not good enough" as you are? So often we try to find reasons that "make sense to us" for why we are not loved and accepted just as we are.

Because of the fashion industry's obsession with slenderness, many women who have as their main message, "I am not good enough. What's the use," will use their bodies as a focal point for self-hatred. On one level they are saying, "If I were only thin enough, then they would love me." But it doesn't work.

Nothing works from the outside. Self-approval and self-acceptance are the key.

ARTHRITIS is a disease that comes from a constant pattern of criticism. First of all, criticism of the self, and then criticism of other people. Arthritic people often attract a lot of criticism because it is their pattern to criticize. They are cursed with "perfectionism," the need to be perfect at all times in every situation.

Do you know of anyone on this planet who is "perfect"? I do not. Why do we set up standards that say we have to be "Super Person," in order to be barely acceptable? It's such a strong expression of "not being good enough," and such a heavy burden to carry.

ASTHMA we call "smother love." There is a feeling that you do not have the right to breathe for yourself. Asthmatic children often have "overdeveloped consciences." They take on guilt feelings for whatever seems wrong in their environment. They feel "unworthy," therefore guilty, and in need of self-punishment.

Geographic cures sometimes work with asthma, especially if the family does *not* go along.

Usually, asthmatic children will "outgrow" their disease. This really means they go away to school, get married, or leave home somehow, and the disease dissolves. Oftentimes, later in life, an experience will happen that pushes an old button within them, and they have another attack. When that happens they are not really responding to the current circumstance, but rather to what used to go on in their childhood.

BOILS AND BURNS, CUTS, FEVERS, SORES, "ITIS," AND INFLAMATIONS all are indications of anger expressing in the body. Anger will find its way to express, no matter *how* much we try to suppress it. Steam that is built up must be released. We fear our anger lest we destroy our world, yet anger can be released as simply as saying, "I am angry about this." True, we can't always say this to our bosses. We can, however, beat the bed or scream in the car or play tennis. These are harmless ways of physically releasing anger.

Spiritual people often believe they "shouldn't" get angry. True, we are all working toward the time when we no longer blame others for our feelings; but until we arrive there, it is healthier to acknowledge what we do feel in the moment.

CANCER is a disease caused by deep resentment held for a long time until it literally eats away at the body. Something happens in childhood that destroys the sense of trust. This experience is never forgotten; and the individual lives with a sense of self-pity, finding it hard to develop and maintain long-term, meaningful relationships. Because of that belief system, life seems to be a series of disappointments. A feeling of hopelessness and helplessness and loss permeates the thinking, and it becomes easy to blame others for all our problems. People with cancer are also very self-critical. To me, learning to love and accept the self is the key to healing cancers.

OVERWEIGHT represents a need for protection. We seek protection from hurts, slights, criticism, abuse, sexuality, and sexual advances; from a fear of life in general and also specifically. Take your choice.

I am not a heavy person, yet I have learned over the years that when I am feeling insecure and not at ease, I will put on a few pounds. When the threat is gone, the excess weight goes away by itself.

Fighting fat is a waste of time and energy. Diets don't work. The minute you stop, the weight goes back up. Loving and approving of yourself, trusting in the process of life and feeling safe because you know the power of your own mind make up the best diet I know of. Go on a diet from negative thoughts, and your weight will take care of itself.

Too many parents stuff food in a baby's mouth no matter what the problem is. These babies grow up to stand in front of an open refrigerator saying, "I don't know what I want," whenever there is a problem.

PAIN of any sort, to me, is an indication of guilt. Guilt always seeks punishment, and punishment creates pain. Chronic pain comes from chronic guilt, often so deeply buried that we are not even aware of it anymore.

Guilt is a totally useless emotion. It never makes anyone feel better nor does it change a situation.

Your "sentence" is now over, so let yourself out of prison. Forgiving is only giving up, letting go.

STROKES are blood clots; congestion in the blood stream in the area of the brain cutting off the blood supply to the brain.

The brain is the computer of the body. Blood is joy. The veins and arteries are channels of joy. Everything works under the law and the action of love. There is love in every bit of intelligence in the Universe. It is impossible to work and function well without love and joy being experienced.

Negative thinking clogs up the brain, and there is no room for love and joy to flow in its free and open way.

Laughter cannot flow if it is not allowed to be free and foolish. It is the same with love and joy. Life is not grim unless we make it so, unless we choose to look at it in that way. We can find total disaster in the smallest upset, and we can find some joy in the greatest tragedy. It is up to us.

Sometimes we try to force our life to go in a certain way when it is not for our highest good. Sometimes we create strokes to force us to go in a totally different direction, to reevaluate our lifestyle.

STIFFNESS in the body represents stiffness in the mind. Fear makes us cling to old ways, and we find it difficult to be flexible. If we believe there is "only one way" to do something, we often find ourselves becoming stiff. We can always find another way to do things. Remember Virginia Satir and her 256 different ways to do dishes.

Notice where in the body the stiffness occurs, look it up on my list of mental patterns, and it will show you where in your mind you are being stiff and rigid.

SURGERY has its place. It is good for broken bones and accidents and for conditions beyond the abilities of a beginner to dissolve. It may be easier under these conditions to have the operation and concentrate all the mental healing work on seeing that the condition is not recreated.

More and more each day there are many wonderful people in the medical profession who are truly dedicated to helping humanity. More and more doctors are turning to holistic ways of healing, treating the whole person. Yet most doctors do not work with the *cause* of any illness; they only treat the symptoms, the effects.

They do this in one of two ways: they poison or they mutilate. Surgeons cut, and if you go to surgeons, they will usually recommend cutting. However, if the decision for surgery is made, prepare yourself for this experience so it will go as smoothly as possible and you will heal as rapidly as possible.

Ask the surgeon and staff to cooperate with you in this. Surgeons and their staffs in the operating rooms are often unaware that even though the patient is unconscious, he or she is still hearing and picking up everything said on a subconscious level.

I heard one New Age leader say she needed some emergency surgery and, before the operation she had a talk with the surgeon and the anesthesiologist. She asked them please to play soft music during the operation and for them to talk to her and each other continuously in positive affirmations. She had the nurse in the recovery room do the same thing, and the operation went easily and her recovery was rapid and comfortable.

With my own clients I always suggest they affirm that, "Every hand that touches me in the hospital is a healing hand and expresses only love," and, "The operation goes quickly and easily and perfectly." Another is, "I am totally comfortable at all times."

After the surgery, have some soft and pleasant music playing as much as possible, and affirm to yourself, "I am healing rapidly, comfortably and perfectly." Tell yourself, "Every day I feel better and better."

If you can, make yourself a tape of a series of positive affirmations. Take your tape recorder to the hospital and play over and over while you rest and recuperate. Notice sensations, not pain. Imagine love flowing from your own heart down through your arms and into your hands. Place your hands over the part that is healing and say to this place, " I love you, and I am helping you to get well."

SWELLING of the body represents clogging and stagnation in the emotional thinking. We create situations where we get "hurt," and we cling to these memories. Swelling often represents bottled-up tears, feeling stuck and trapped, or blaming others for our own limitations.

Release the past, let it wash away. Take back your own power. Stop dwelling on what you don't want. Use your mind to create what you "do want." Let yourself flow with the tide of life.

TUMORS are false growths. An oyster takes a tiny grain of sand and, to protect itself, grows a hard and shiny shell around it. We call it a pearl and think it is beautiful.

We take an old hurt and nurse it and keep pulling the scab off it, and in time we have a tumor.

I call this running the old movie. I believe the reason women have so many tumors in the uterus area is that they take an emotional hurt, a blow to their femininity, and nurse it. I call this the "He done me wrong," syndrome.

Just because a relationship ends does not mean there is something wrong with us, nor does it lesson our self-worth.

It is not *what happens,* it is how we *react* to it. We are each 100% responsible for all our experiences. What beliefs about yourself do you need to change in order to attract more loving kinds of behavior?

In the infinity of life where I am,
all is perfect, whole and complete.
I recognize my body as a good friend.
Each cell in my body has Divine Intelligence.
I listen to what it tells me,
and know that its advice is valid.
I am always safe, and Divinely protected and guided.
I choose to be healthy and free.
All is well in my world.

 *Chapter Fifteen*
THE LIST

"I am healthy, whole and complete."

As you look through the following list taken from my book *HEAL YOUR BODY,* see if you can find the correlation between diseases you may have had or are having now and the probable causes I have listed.

A good way to use this list when you have a physical problem:

1. Look up the mental cause. See if this could be true for you. If not, sit quietly and ask yourself, "What could be the thoughts in me that created this?"

2. Repeat to yourself, "I am willing to release the pattern in my consciousness that has created this condition."

3. Repeat the new thought pattern to yourself several times.

4. Assume that you are already in the process of healing.

Whenever you think of the condition, repeat the steps.

Problem	Probable Cause	New Thought Pattern
Abdominal Cramps	Fear. Stopping the process.	I trust the process of life. I am safe.
Abscess	Fermenting thoughts over hurts, slights and revenge.	I allow my thoughts to be free. The past is over. I am at peace.
Accidents	Inability to speak up for the self. Rebellion against authority. Belief in violence.	I release the pattern in me that created this. I am at peace. I am worthwhile.
Aches	Longing for love. Longing to be held.	I love and approve of myself. I am loving and lovable.
Acne	Not accepting the self. Dislike of the self.	I am a Divine expression of life. I love and accept myself where I am right now.
Addictions	Running from the self. Fear. Not knowing how to love the self.	I now discover how wonderful I am. I choose to love and enjoy myself.
Addison's Disease	Severe emotional malnutrition. Anger at the self.	I lovingly take care of my body, my mind and my emotions.
Adenoids	Family friction, arguments. Child feeling unwelcome, in the way.	This child is wanted and welcomed and deeply loved.
Adrenal Problems	Defeatism. No longer caring for the self. Anxiety.	I love and approve of myself. It is safe for me to care for myself.

Aging Problems	Social beliefs. Old thinking. Fear of being one's self. Rejection of the now.	*I love and accept myself at every age. Each moment in life is perfect.*
AIDS	Denial of the self. Sexual guilt. A strong belief in not being "good enough."	*I am a Divine, magnificent expression of life. I rejoice in my sexuality. I rejoice in all that I am. I love myself.*
Alcoholism	What's the use? Feeling of futility, guilt, inadequacy. Self-rejection.	*I live in the now. Each moment is new. I choose to see my self-worth. I love and approve of myself.*
Allergies	Who are you allergic to? Denying your own power.	*The world is safe and friendly. I am safe. I am at peace with life.*
Alzheimer's Disease	A desire to leave the planet. The inability to face life as it is.	*Everything happens in the right time-space sequence. Divine right action is taking place at all times.*
Amnesia	Fear. Running from life. Inability to stand up for the self.	*Intelligence, courage and self-worth are always present. It is safe to be alive.*
Anemia	"Yes-but" attitude. Lack of joy. Fear of life. Feeling not good enough.	*It is safe for me to experience joy in every area of my life. I love life.*
Ankle	Represents mobility and direction.	*I move forward easily in life.*
Anorectal Bleeding	Anger and frustration.	*I trust the process of life. Only right and good action is taking place in my life.*

Anorexia	Denying the self life. Extreme fear, self-hatred and rejection.	*It is safe to be me. I am wonderful just as I am. I choose to live. I choose joy and self-acceptance.*
Anus	Releasing point. Dumping ground.	*I easily and comfortably release that which I no longer need in life.*
– Abscess	Anger in relation to what you don't want to release.	*It is safe to let go. Only that which I no longer need leaves my body.*
– Bleeding	See Anorectal Bleeding	
– Fistula	Incomplete releasing of trash. Holding on to garbage of the past.	*It is with love that I totally release the past. I am free. I am love.*
– Itching	Guilt over the past. Remorse.	*I lovingly forgive myself. I am free.*
– Pain	Guilt. Desire for punishment. Not good enough.	*The past is over. I choose to love and approve of myself in the now.*
Anxiety	Not trusting the flow and the process of life.	*I love and approve of myself, and I trust the process of life. I am safe.*
Apathy	Resistance to feeling. Deadening of the self. Fear.	*It is safe to feel. I open myself to life. I am willing to experience life.*
Appendicitis	Fear. Fear of life. Blocking the flow of good.	*I am safe. I relax and let life flow joyously.*

Appetite		
– Excessive	Fear. Needing protection. Judging the emotions.	*I am safe. It is safe to feel. My feelings are normal and acceptable.*
– Loss of	Fear. Protecting the self. Not trusting life.	*I love and approve of myself. I am safe. Life is safe and joyous.*
Arms	Represent the capacity and ability to hold the experiences of life.	*I lovingly hold and embrace my experiences with ease and with joy.*
Arteriosclerosis	Resistance, tension. Hardened narrow-mindedness. Refusing to see good.	*I am completely open to life and to joy. I choose to see with love.*
Arteries	Carry the joy of life.	*I am filled with joy. It flows through me with every beat of my heart.*
Arthritis	Feeling unloved. Criticism, resentment.	*I am love. I now choose to love and approve of myself. I see others with love.*
Arthritic Fingers	A desire to punish. Blame. Feeling victimized.	*I see with love and understanding. I hold all my experiences up to the light of love.*
Asphyxiating Attacks	Fear. Not trusting the process of life. Getting stuck in childhood.	*It is safe to grow up. The world is safe. I am safe.*

Asthma	Smother love. Inability to breathe for one's self. Feeling stifled. Suppressed crying.	*It is safe now for me to take charge of my own life. I choose to be free.*
Athlete's Foot	Frustration at not being accepted. Inability to move forward with ease.	*I love and approve of myself. I give myself permission to go ahead. It's safe to move.*
Baby Asthma	Fear of life. Not wanting to be here.	*This child is safe and loved. This child is welcomed and cherished.*
Backs	Represent the support of life.	*I know that life always supports me.*
Back Problems		
– Upper	Lack of emotional support. Feeling unloved. Holding back love.	*I love and approve of myself. Life supports and loves me.*
– Middle	Guilt. Stuck in all that "stuff" back there. Get off my back.	*I release the past. I am free to move forward with love in my heart.*
– Lower	Fear of money. Lack of financial support.	*I trust the process of life. All I need is always taken care of. I am safe.*
Bad Breath	Anger and revenge thoughts. Experiences backing up.	*I release the past with love. I choose to voice only love.*

Balance, Loss of	Scattered thinking. Not centered.	*I center myself in safety and accept the perfection of my life. All is well.*
Baldness	Fear. Tension. Trying to control everything. Not trusting the process of life.	*I am safe. I love and approve of myself. I trust life.*
Bedwetting	Fear of parent, usually the father.	*This child is seen with love, with compassion, and with understanding. All is well.*
Belching	Fear. Gulping life too quickly.	*There is time and space for everything I need to do. I am at peace.*
Birth Defects	Karmic. You selected to come that way. We choose our parents.	*Every experience is perfect for our growth process. I am at peace with where I am.*
Blackheads	Feeling dirty and unloved.	*I love and approve of myself. I am loving and lovable.*
Bladder Problems	Anxiety. Holding on to old ideas. Fear of letting go. Being "pissed off."	*I comfortably and easily release the old and welcome the new in my life. I am safe.*
Bleeding	Joy running out. Anger. But where?	*I am the joy of life expressing and receiving in perfect rhythm.*
Bleeding Gums	Lack of joy in the decisions made in life.	*I trust that right action is always taking place in my life. I am at peace.*

Blisters	Resistance. Lack of emotional protection.	*I gently flow with life and each new experience. All is well.*
Blood	Represents joy in the body, flowing freely.	*I am the joy of life expressing and receiving.*
Blood Problems	Lack of joy. Lack of circulation of ideas.	*Joyous new ideas are circulating freely within me.*
– Anemic	See Anemia	
– Clotting	Closing down the flow of joy.	*I awaken new life within me. I flow.*
Blood Pressure		
– High	Longstanding emotional problem not solved.	*I joyously release the past. I am at peace.*
– Low	Lack of love as a child. Defeatism. What's the use; it won't work anyway.	*I now choose to live in the ever-joyous NOW. My life is a joy.*
Body Odor	Fear. Dislike of the self. Fear of others.	*I love and approve of myself. I am safe.*
Boils	Anger. Boiling over. Seething.	*I express love and joy, and I am at peace.*
Bones	Represent the structure of the Universe.	*I am well structured and balanced.*

Bone Problems		
– Breaks	Rebelling against authority.	*In my world, I am my own authority; for I am the only one who thinks in my mind.*
– Deformity	Mental pressure and tightness. Muscles can't stretch. Loss of mental mobility.	*I breathe in life fully. I relax and trust the flow and the process of life.*
Bowels	Represent the release of waste.	*Letting go is easy.*
– Problems	Fear of letting go of the old and no longer needed.	*I freely and easily release the old and joyously welcome the new.*
Brain	Represents the computer, the switchboard.	*I am the loving operator of my mind.*
– Tumor	Incorrect computerized beliefs. Stubborn. Refusing to change old patterns.	*It is easy for me to reprogram the computer of my mind. All of life is change, and my mind is ever new.*
Breasts	Represent mothering and nurturing.	*I take in and give out nourishment in perfect balance.*
Breast Problems		
– Cysts, Lumps, Soreness	Overmothering. Overprotection. Overbearing attitudes. Cutting off nourishment.	*I am free to be me, and I allow others the freedom to be who they are. It is safe for all of us to grow up.*

Breath	Represents the ability to take in life.	*I love life.*
Breathing Problems	Fear or refusal to take in life fully. Not feeling the right to take up space or even to exist at times.	*It is my birthright to live life fully and freely. I am worth loving. I now choose to live life fully.*
Bright's Disease	Feeling like a kid who "can't do it right," and is "not good enough." A failure. Loss.	*I love and approve of myself. I care for me. I am totally adequate at all times.*
Bronchitis	Inflamed family environment. Arguments and yelling. Sometimes silent.	*I declare peace and harmony within me and around me. All is well.*
Bruises	The little bumps in life. Self-punishment.	*I love and cherish myself. I am kind and gentle with me. All is well.*
Burns	Anger. Burning up. Incensed.	*I create only peace and harmony within myself and in my environment. I deserve to feel good.*
Bursitis	Repressed anger. Wanting to hit someone.	*Love relaxes and releases all unlike itself.*
Buttocks	Represent power. Loose buttocks, loss of power.	*I use my power wisely. I am strong. I feel safe. All is well.*
Callouses	Hardened concepts and ideas. Fear solidified.	*It is safe to see and experience new ideas and new ways. I am open and receptive to good.*

Cancer	Deep hurt. Longstanding resentment. Deep secret or grief eating away at the self. Carrying hatreds. What's the use.	I lovingly forgive and release all of the past. I choose to fill my world with joy. I love and approve of myself.
Candidiasis	Feeling very scattered. Lots of frustration and anger. Demanding and untrusting in relationships. Great takers.	I give myself permission to be all that I can be and I deserve the very best in life. I love and appreciate myself and others.
Canker Sores	Festering words held back by the lips. Blame.	I create only joyful experiences in my loving world.
Carbuncle	Poisonous anger about personal injustices.	I release the past and allow time to heal every area of my life.
Car Sickness	Fear. Bondage. Feeling of being trapped.	I move with ease through time and space. Only love surrounds me.
Cataracts	Inability to see ahead with joy. Dark future.	Life is eternal and filled with joy. I look forward to every moment.
Cellulite	Getting stuck in early childhood pain. Holding onto the lumps and bumps of the past. Difficulty in moving forward. Fear of choosing your own direction.	I forgive everyone. I forgive myself. I forgive all past experiences. I am free.
Childhood Diseases	Belief in calendars and social concepts and false laws. Childish behavior in the adults around them.	This child is Divinely protected and surrounded by love. We claim mental immunity.

Chills	Mental contraction, pulling away and in. Desire to retreat. Leave me alone.	*I am safe and secure at all times. Love surrounds me and protects me. All is well.*
Cholesterol	Clogging the channels of joy. Fear of accepting joy.	*I choose to love life. My channels of joy are wide open. It is safe to receive.*
Chronic Diseases	A refusal to change. Fear of the future. Not feeling safe.	*I am willing to change and to grow. I now create a safe new future.*
Colds	Too much going on at once. Mental confusion, disorder. Small hurts. "I get three colds every winter," type of belief.	*I allow my mind to relax and be at peace. Clarity and harmony are within me and around me.*
Colic	Mental irritation, impatience, annoyance in the surroundings.	*This child responds only to love and to loving thoughts. All is peaceful.*
Colitis	Overexacting parents. Feeling of oppression and defeat. Great need for affection.	*I love and approve of myself. I create my own joy. I choose to be a winner in life.*
Coma	Fear. Escaping something or someone.	*We surround you with safety and love. We create a space for you to heal. You are love.*
Conjunctivitis	Anger and frustration at what you are looking at in life.	*I see with eyes of love. There is a harmonious solution, and I accept it now.*

Constipation	Refusing to release old ideas. Stuck in the past. Sometimes stinginess.	*As I release the past, the new and fresh and vital enter. I allow life to flow through me.*
Coronary Thrombosis	Feeling alone and scared. Not good enough. Don't do enough. Will never make it.	*I am one with all of life. The Universe totally supports me. All is well.*
Cramps	Tension. Fear. Gripping, holding on.	*I relax and allow my mind to be peaceful.*
Croup	See Bronchitis	
Crying	Tears are the river of life. Shed in joy as well as in sadness and fear.	*I am peaceful with all of my emotions. I love and approve of myself.*
Cushing's Disease	Mental imbalance. Overproduction of crushing ideas. A feeling of being over-powered.	*I lovingly balance my mind and my body. I now choose thoughts that make me feel good.*
Cysts	Running the old painful movie. Nursing hurts. A false growth.	*The movies of my mind are beautiful because I choose to make them so. I love me.*
Cystic Fibrosis	A thick belief that life won't work for you. Poor me.	*Life loves me, and I love life. I now choose to take in life fully and freely.*

Deafness	Rejection, stubbornness, isolation. What don't you want to hear? Don't bother me.	*I listen to the Divine and rejoice at all that I am able to hear. I am one with all.*
Diabetes	Longing for what might have been. A great need to control. Deep sorrow. No sweetness left.	*This moment is filled with joy. I now choose to experience the sweetness of today.*
Diarrhea	Fear. Rejection. Running off.	*My intake, assimilation and elimination are in perfect order. I am at peace with life.*
Dizziness	Flighty, scattered thinking. A refusal to look.	*I am deeply centered and peaceful in life. It is safe for me to be alive and joyous.*
Ears	Represent the capacity to hear.	*I hear with love.*
Earache	Anger. Not wanting to hear. Too much turmoil. Parents arguing.	*Harmony surrounds me. I listen with love to the pleasant and the good. I am a center for love.*
Eczema	Breath-taking antagonism. Mental erruptions.	*Harmony and peace, love and joy surround me and indwell me. I am safe and secure.*
Edema	What or who won't you let go of?	*I willingly release the past. It is safe for me to let go. I am free now.*

Elbow	Represents changing directions and accepting new experiences.	I easily flow with new experiences, with new directions and new changes.
Emphysema	Fear of taking in life. Not worthy of living.	It is my birthright to live fully and freely. I love life. I love me.
Epilepsy	Sense of persecution. Rejection of life. A feeling of great struggle. Self-violence.	I choose to see life as eternal and joyous. I am eternal and joyous and at peace.
Eyes	Represent the capacity to see clearly — past, present and future.	I see with love and joy.
Eye Problems	Not liking what you see in your own life.	I now create a life I love to look at.
– Astigmatism	"I trouble." Fear of really seeing the self.	I am now willing to see my own beauty and magnificence.
– Cataracts	Inability to see ahead with joy. Dark future.	Life is eternal and filled with joy.
– Children	Not wanting to see what is going on in the family.	Harmony and joy and beauty and safety now surround this child.
– Crossed	Not wanting to see what's out there. Crossed purposes.	It is safe for me to see. I am at peace.
– Farsighted	Fear of the present.	I am safe in the here and now. I see that.

– Glaucoma	Stony unforgiveness. Pressure from long-standing hurts. Overwhelmed by it all.	*I see with love and tenderness.*
– Nearsighted	Fear of the future.	*I accept Divine guidance and am always safe.*
– Wall Eyed	Fear of looking at the present, right here.	*I love and approve of myself right now.*
Face	Represents what we show the world.	*It is safe to be me. I express who I am.*
Fainting	Fear. Can't cope. Blacking out.	*I have the power and strength and knowledge to handle everything in my life.*
Fat	Represents protection. Oversensitivity.	*I am protected by Divine love. I am always safe and secure.*
Fatigue	Resistance, boredom. Lack of love for what one does.	*I am enthusiastic about life and filled with energy and enthusiasm.*
Feet	Represent our understanding — of ourselves, of life, of others.	*My understanding is clear, and I am willing to change with the times. I am safe.*
Female Problems	Denial of the self. Rejecting femininity. Rejection of the feminine principle.	*I rejoice in my femaleness. I love being a woman. I love my body.*

Fevers	Anger. Burning up.	I am the cool, calm, expression of peace and love.
Fibroid Tumors and Cysts	Nursing a hurt from a partner. A blow to the feminine ego.	I release the pattern in me that attracted this experience. I create only good in my life.
Fingers	Represent the details of life.	I am peaceful with the details of life.
– Thumb	Represents intellect and worry.	My mind is at peace.
– Index Finger	Represents ego and fear.	I am secure.
– Middle Finger	Represents anger and sexuality.	I am comfortable with my sexuality.
– Ring Finger	Represents unions and grief.	I am peacefully loving.
– Little Finger	Represents the family and pretending.	I am myself with the family of life.
Fistula	Fear. A blockage in the letting go process.	I am safe. I trust fully in the process of life. Life is for me.
Flu	See Influenza	
Foot Problems	Fear of the future and of not stepping forward in life.	I move forward in life with joy and with ease.
Frigidity	Fear. Denial of pleasure. A belief that sex is bad. Insensitive partners.	It is safe for me to enjoy my own body. I rejoice in being a woman.

Gallstones	Bitterness. Hard thoughts. Condemning. Pride.	*There is joyous release of the past. Life is sweet, and so am I.*
Gangrene	Mental morbidity. Drowning of joy with poisonous thoughts.	*I now choose harmonious thoughts and let the joy flow freely through me.*
Gas Pains	Gripping. Fear. Undigested ideas.	*I relax and let life flow through me with ease.*
Gastritis	Prolonged uncertainty. A feeling of doom.	*I love and approve of myself. I am safe.*
Genitals	Represent the masculine and feminine principles.	*It is safe to be who I am.*
– Problems	Worry about not being good enough.	*I rejoice in my own expression of life. I am perfect just as I am. I love and approve of myself.*
Glands	Represent holding stations. Self-starting activity.	*I am the creative power in my world.*
Glandular Problems	Poor distribution of get-up-and-go ideas.	*I have all the Divine ideas and activity I need. I move forward right now.*
Goiter	Hatred for being inflicted upon. Victim. Feeling thwarted in life. Unfulfilled.	*I am the power and authority in my life. I am free to be me.*

Gout	The need to dominate. Impatience, anger.	*I am safe and secure. I am at peace with myself and with others.*
Gray Hair	Stress. A belief in pressure and strain.	*I am at peace and comfortable in every area of my life. I am strong and capable.*
Growths	Nursing those old hurts. Building resentment.	*I easily forgive. I love myself and will reward myself with thoughts of praise.*
Gum Problems	Inability to back up decisions. Wishy-washy about life.	*I am a decisive person. I follow through and support myself with love.*
Halitosis	Rotten attitudes, vile gossip, foul thinking.	*I speak with gentleness and love. I exhale only the good.*
Hands	Hold and handle. Clutch and grip. Grasping and letting go. Caressing. Pinching. All ways of dealing with experiences.	*I choose to handle all my experiences with love and with joy and with ease.*
Hay Fever	Emotional congestion. Fear of the calendar. A belief in persecution. Guilt.	*I am one with ALL OF LIFE. I am safe at all times.*
Headaches	Invalidating the self. Self-criticism. Fear.	*I love and approve of myself. I see myself and what I do with eyes of love. I am safe.*
Heartburn	Fear. Fear. Fear. Clutching fear.	*I breathe freely and fully. I am safe. I trust the process of life.*

Heart	Represents the center of love and security. (See Blood)	*My heart beats to the rhythm of love.*
– Problems	Longstanding emotional problems. Lack of joy. Hardening of the heart. Belief in strain and stress.	*Joy. Joy. Joy. I lovingly allow joy to flow through my mind and body and experience.*
– Attack	Squeezing all the joy out of the heart in favor of money or position, etc.	*I bring joy back to the center of my heart. I express love to all.*
Hemorrhoids	Fear of deadlines. Anger of the past. Afraid to let go. Feeling burdened.	*I release all that is unlike love. There is time and space for everything I want to do.*
Hepatitis	Resistance to change. Fear, anger, hatred. Liver is the seat of anger and rage.	*My mind is cleansed and free. I leave the past and move into the new. All is well.*
Hernia	Ruptured relationships. Strain, burdens. Incorrect creative expression.	*My mind is gentle and harmonious. I love and approve of myself. I am free to be me.*
Herpes	Mass belief in sexual guilt and the need for punishment. Public shame. Belief in a punishing God. Rejection of the genitals.	*My concept of God supports me. I am normal and natural. I rejoice in my own sexuality and in my own body. I am wonderful.*

Hip	Carries the body in perfect balance. Major thrust in moving forward.	*Hip Hip Hooray — there is joy in every day.*
Hip Problems	Fear of going forward in major decisions. Nothing to move foward to.	*I am in perfect balance. I move forward in life with ease and with joy at every age.*
Hives	Small hidden fears. Mountains out of molehills.	*I bring peace to every corner of my life.*
Hodgkin's Disease	Blame and a tremendous fear of "not being good enough." A frantic race to prove one's self until the blood has no substance left to support itself. The joy of life is forgotten in the race for acceptance.	*I am perfectly happy to be me. I am good enough just as I am. I love and approve of myself. I am joy expressing and receiving.*
Holding Fluids	What are you afraid of losing?	*I willingly release with joy.*
Hyperglycemia	See Diabetes	
Hyperthyroidism	Extreme disappointment at not being able to do what you want to do. Always fulfilling others, not the self.	*I return my power to its rightful place. I make my own decisions. I fulfill myself.*
Hyperventilation	Fear. Resisting change. Not trusting the process.	*I am safe everywhere in the Universe. I love myself and trust the process of life.*

Hypoglycemia	Overwhelmed by the burdens in life. What's the use?	I now choose to make my life light and easy and joyful.
Ileitis	Fear. Worry. Not being good enough.	I love and approve of myself. I am doing the best I can. I am wonderful. I am at peace.
Impotence	Sexual pressure, tension, guilt. Social beliefs. Spite against a previous mate. Fear of mother.	I now allow the full power of my sexual principle to operate with ease and with joy.
Incontinence	A letting go. A feeling of being out of control emotionally. A lack of self nourishment.	As I nurture myself, those around me are nurtured. I am gentle and caring with myself. All is well.
Incurable	Cannot be cured by outer means at this point. We must "go within" to effect the cure. It came from nowhere and will go back to nowhere.	Miracles happen every day. I go within to dissolve the pattern that created this, and I now accept a Divine healing. And so it is!
Indigestion	Gut-level fear, dread, anxiety. Griping and grunging.	I digest and assimilate all new experiences peacefully and joyously.
Infection	Irritation, anger, annoyance.	I choose to be peaceful and harmonious.
Inflammation "Itis"	Fear. Seeing red. Inflamed thinking.	My thinking is peaceful, calm and centered.

Influenza	Response to mass negativity and beliefs. Fear. Belief in statistics.	*I am beyond group beliefs or the calendar. I am free from all congestion and influence.*
Ingrown Toenail	Worry and guilt about your right to move forward.	*It is my Divine right to take my own direction in life. I am safe. I am free.*
Insanity	Fleeing from the family. Escapism, withdrawal. Violent separation from life.	*This mind knows its true identity and is a creative point of Divine Self-Expression.*
Insomnia	Fear. Not trusting the process of life. Guilt.	*I lovingly release the day and slip into peaceful sleep, knowing tomorrow will take care of itself.*
Itching	Desires that go against the grain. Unsatisfied. Remorse. Itching to get out or get away.	*I am at peace just where I am. I accept my good, knowing all my needs and desires will be fulfilled.*
"Itis"	Anger and frustration about conditions you are looking at in your own life.	*I am willing to change all patterns of criticism. I love and approve of myself.*
Jaundice	Internal and external prejudice. Unbalanced reason.	*I feel tolerance and compassion and love for all people, myself included.*
Jaw Problems	Anger. Resentment. Desire for revenge.	*I am willing to change the patterns in me that created this condition. I love and approve of myself. I am safe.*

Joints	Represent changes in direction in life and the ease of these movements.	*I easily flow with change. My life is Divinely guided, and I am always going in the best direction.*
Keratitis	Extreme anger. A desire to hit those or what you see.	*I allow the love from my own heart to heal all that I see. I choose peace. All is well in my world.*
Kidney Problems	Criticism, diappointment, failure. Shame. Reacting like a little kid.	*Divine right action is always taking place in my life. Only good comes from each experience. It is safe to grow up.*
Knee	Represents pride and ego.	*I am flexible and flowing.*
– Problems	Stubborn ego and pride. Inability to bend. Fear. Inflexibility. Won't give in.	*Forgiveness. Understanding. Compassion. I bend and flow with ease, and all is well.*
Laryngitis	So mad you can't speak. Fear of speaking up. Resentment of authority	*I am free to ask for what I want. It is safe to express myself. I am at peace.*
Legs	Carry us forward in life.	*Life is for me.*
Leg Problems		
– Upper	Holding on to old childhood traumas.	*They were doing the best they could with the understanding, awareness and knowledge they had. I set them free.*

– Lower	Fear of the future. Not wanting to move.	*I move forward with confidence and joy, knowing that all is well in my future.*
Leprosy	Inability to handle life at all. A long belief in not being good enough or clean enough.	*I rise above all limitations. I am Divinely guided and inspired. Love heals all life.*
Leukorrhea	A belief that women are powerless over the opposite sex. Anger at a mate.	*I create all my experiences. I am the power. I rejoice in my femaleness. I am free.*
Leukemia	Brutally killing inspiration. What's the use?	*I move beyond past limitations into the freedom of the now. It is safe to be me.*
Liver	Seat of anger and primitive emotions.	*Love and peace and joy are what I know.*
– Problems	Chronic complaining. Justifying fault-finding to deceive yourself. Feeling bad.	*I choose to live through the open space in my heart. I look for love and find it everywhere.*
Lockjaw	Anger. A desire to control. A refusal to express feelings.	*I trust the process of life. I easily ask for what I want. Life supports me.*
Lump in Throat	Fear. Not trusting the process of life.	*I am safe. I trust that life is here for me. I express myself freely and joyously.*
Lung	The ability to take in life.	*I take in life in perfect balance.*

– Problems	Depression. Grief. Fear of taking in life. Not worthy of living fully.	*I have the capacity to take in the fullness of life. I lovingly live life to the fullest.*
Lupus	A giving up. Better to die than stand up for one's self. Anger and punishment.	*I speak up for myself freely and easily. I claim my own power. I love and approve of myself. I am free and safe.*
Lymph Problems	A warning that the mind needs to be re-centered on the essentials of life. Love and joy.	*I am now totally centered in the love and joy of being alive. I flow with life. Peace of mind is mine.*
Mastoiditis	Anger and frustration. A desire not to hear what is going on. Usually in children. Fear infecting the understanding.	*Divine peace and harmony surround and indwell me. I am an oasis of peace and love and joy. All is well in my world.*
Menopause Problems	Fear of no longer being wanted. Fear of aging. Self-rejection. Not being good enough.	*I am balanced and peaceful in all changes of cycles, and I bless my body with love.*
Menstrual Problems	Rejection of one's feminity. Guilt, fear. Belief that the genitals are sinful or dirty.	*I accept my full power as a woman and accept all my bodily processes as normal and natural. I love and approve of myself.*
Migraine Headaches	Dislike against being driven. Resisting the flow of life. Sexual fears. (Can usually be relieved by masturbation.)	*I relax into the flow of life and let life provide all that I need easily and comfortably. Life is for me.*

Miscarriage	Fear. Fear of the future. Not now — later. Inappropriate timing.	*Divine right action is always taking place in my life. I love and approve of myself. All is well.*
Mononucleosis	A pattern of belittling life. Making others wrong. Lots of inner criticism. A habit of playing "Ain't it awful."	*I am one with all of life. I see myself in others and I love what I see. I rejoice in being alive.*
Motion Sickness	Fear. Fear of not being in control.	*I am always in control of my thoughts. I am safe. I love and approve of myself.*
Mouth	Represents taking in of new ideas and nourishment.	*I nourish myself with love.*
— Problems	Set opinions. Closed mind. Incapacity to take in new ideas.	*I welcome new ideas and new concepts and prepare them for digestion and assimilation.*
Mucus Colon	Layered deposits of old, confused thoughts clogging the channel of elimination. Wallowing in the gummed mire of the past.	*I release and dissolve the past. I am a clear thinker. I live in the now in peace and joy.*
Multiple Sclerosis	Mental hardness, hard-heartedness, iron will, inflexibility. Fear.	*By choosing loving, joyous thoughts, I create a loving, joyous world. I am safe and free.*

176

Muscular Dystrophy	Extreme fear. Frantic desire to control everything and everyone. A deep need to feel safe. Loss of faith and trust.	*It is safe for me to be alive. It is safe to be me. I am good enough as I am. I trust myself.*
Myopia	Fear of the future. Not trusting what is ahead.	*I trust the process of life. I am safe.*
Nails	Represent protection.	*I reach out safely.*
Nail Biting	Frustration. Eating away at the self. Spite of a parent.	*It is safe for me to grow up. I now handle my own life with joy and with ease.*
Narcolepsy	Can't cope. Extreme fear. Wanting to get away from it all. Don't want to be here.	*I rely on Divine wisdom and guidance to protect me at all times. I am safe.*
Nausea	Fear. Rejecting an idea or experience.	*I am safe. I trust the process of life to bring only good to me.*
Nearsightedness	See Myopia	
Neck	Represents flexibility. The ability to see what's back there.	*I am peaceful with life.*
Neck Problems	Refusing to see other sides of a question. Stubbornness, inflexibility.	*It is with flexibility and ease that I see all sides of an issue. There are endless ways of doing things and seeing things. I am safe.*

Nephritis	Overreaction to disappointment and failure.	*Only right action is taking place in my life. I release the old and welcome the new. All is well.*
Nerves	Represent communication. Receptive reporters.	*I communicate with ease and with joy.*
Nervous Breakdown	Self-centeredness. Jamming the channels of communication.	*I open my heart and create only loving communication. I am safe. I am well.*
Nervousness	Fear, anxiety, struggle, rushing. Not trusting the process of life.	*I am on an endless journey through eternity, and there is plenty of time. I communicate with my heart. All is well.*
Neuralgia	Punishment for guilt. Anguish over communication.	*I forgive myself. I love and approve of myself. I communicate with love.*
Nodules	Resentment and frustration and hurt ego over career.	*I release the pattern of delay within me, and I now allow success to be mine.*
Nose	Represents self-recognition.	*I recognize my own intuitive ability*
Nose Bleeds	A need for recognition. Feeling unrecognized and unnoticed. Crying for love.	*I love and approve of myself. I recognize my own true worth. I am wonderful.*
Numbness	Withholding love and consideration. Going dead mentally.	*I share my feelings and my love. I respond to love in everyone.*

Osteomyelitis	Anger and frustration at the very structure of life. Feeling unsupported.	*I am peaceful with and trust the process of life. I am safe and secure.*
Ovaries	Represent points of creation. Creativity.	*I am balanced in my creative flow.*
Overweight	Fear, need for protection. Running away from feelings. Insecurity, self-rejection. Seeking fulfillment.	*I am at peace with my own feelings. I am safe where I am. I create my own security. I love and approve of myself.*
Pain	Guilt. Guilt always seeks punishment.	*I lovingly release the past. They are free, and I am free. All is well in my heart now.*
Pancreas	Represents the sweetness of life.	*My life is sweet.*
Pancreatitis	Rejection. Anger and frustration because life seems to have lost its sweetness.	*I love and approve of myself, and I alone create sweetness and joy in my life.*
Paralysis	Fear, terror. Escaping a situation or person. Resistance.	*I am one with all of life. I am safe, and I am totally adequate for all situations.*
Parkinson's Disease	Fear and an intense desire to control everything and everyone.	*I relax knowing that I am safe. Life is for me, and I trust the process of life.*
Peptic Ulcer	Fear. A belief that you are not good enough. Anxious to please.	*I love and approve of myself. I am at peace with myself. I am wonderful.*

Petit Mal	See Epilepsy	
Phlebitis	Anger and frustration. Blaming others for the limitation and lack of joy in life.	*Joy now flows freely within me, and I am at peace with life.*
Piles	See Hemorrhoids	
Pink Eye	Anger and frustration. Not wanting to see.	*I release the need to be right. I am at peace. I love and approve of myself.*
Pituitary Gland	Represents the control center.	*My mind and body are in perfect balance. I control my thoughts.*
Plantar Wart	Anger at the very basis of your understanding. Spreading frustration about the future.	*I move forward with confidence and ease. I trust and flow with the process of life.*
Pneumonia	Desperate. Tired of life. Emotional wounds that are not allowed to heal.	*I freely take in Divine ideas that are filled with the breath and the intelligence of life. This is a new moment.*
Polio	Paralyzing jealousy. A desire to stop someone.	*There is enough for everyone. I create my good and my freedom with loving thoughts.*
Post Nasal Drip	Inner crying. Childish tears. Victim.	*I acknowledge and accept that I am the creative power in my world. I now choose to enjoy my life.*

Pre-Menstrual Syndrome – P.M.S.	Allowing confusion to reign. Giving power to outside influences. Rejection of the feminine processes.	I now take charge of my mind and my life. I am a powerful, dynamite woman! Every part of my body functions perfectly. I love me.
Prostate	Represents the masculine principle.	I accept and rejoice in my masculinity.
Prostate Problems	Mental fears weaken the masculinity. Giving up. Sexual pressure and guilt. Belief in aging.	I love and approve of myself. I accept my own power. I am forever young in spirit.
Psoriasis	Fear of being hurt. Deadening the senses and the self. Refusing to accept responsibility for our own feelings.	I am alive to the joys of living. I deserve and accept the very best in life. I love and approve of myself.
Pubic Bone	Represents genital protection.	My sexuality is safe.
Pyorrhea	Anger at the inability to make decisions. Wishy-washy people.	I approve of myself, and my decisions are always perfect for me.
Quinsy	A strong belief that you cannot speak up for yourself and ask for your needs.	It is my birthright to have my needs met. I now ask for what I want with love and with ease.

Rabies	Anger. A belief that violence is the answer.	*I am surrounded and indwelled with peace.*
Rash	Irritation over delays. Babyish way to get attention.	*I love and approve of myself. I am at peace with the process of life.*
Rectum	See Anus	
Rheumatism	Feeling victimized. Lack of love. Chronic bitterness. Resentment.	*I create my own experiences. As I love and approve of myself and others, my experiences get better and better.*
Rheumatoid Arthritis	Deep criticism of authority. Feeling very put upon.	*I am my own authority. I love and approve of myself. Life is good.*
Rickets	Emotional malnutrition. Lack of love and security.	*I am secure and am nourished by the love of the Universe itself.*
Ringworm	Allowing others to get under your skin. Not feeling good enough or clean enough.	*I love and approve of myself. No person, place or thing has any power over me. I am free.*
Round Shoulders	Carrying the burdens of life. Helpless and hopelessness.	*I stand tall and free. I love and approve of me. My life gets better every day.*
Sagging Lines	Sagging lines on the face come from sagging thoughts in the mind. Resentment of life.	*I express the joy of living and allow myself to enjoy every moment of every day totally. I become young again.*

Scabies	Infected thinking. Allowing others to get under your skin.	*I am the living, loving, joyous expression of life. I am my own person.*
Sciatica	Being hypocritical. Fear of money and of the future.	*I move into my greater good. My good is everywhere, and I am secure and safe.*
Scleroderma	Feeling unprotected and unsafe. Feeling irritated and threatened by others. Creating protection.	*I am divinely protected and safe at all times. Everything I do is right and brings me love, which I accept with joy and pleasure.*
Scoliosis	See Round Shoulders	
Seasickness	Fear. Fear of death. Lack of control.	*I am totally safe in the Univese. I am at peace everywhere. I trust life.*
Senility	Returning to the so-called safety of childhood. Demanding care and attention. A form of control of those around you. Escapism.	*Divine protection. Safety. Peace. The Intelligence of the Universe operates at every level of life.*
Shingles	Waiting for the other shoe to drop. Fear and tension. Too sensitive.	*I am relaxed and peaceful because I trust the process of life. All is well in my world.*
Shoulders	Are meant to carry joy, not burdens.	*I am free to be joyous.*

Sickle Cell Anemia	A belief that one is not good enough that destroys the very joy of life.	*This child lives and breathes the joy of life and is nourished by love. God works miracles every day.*
Sinus Problems	Irritation to one person, someone close.	*I declare peace and harmony indwell me and surround me at all times. All is well.*
Skin	Protects our individuality. A sense organ.	*I feel safe to be me.*
Skin Problems	Anxiety, fear. Old, buried guck. I am being threatened.	*I lovingly protect myself with thoughts of joy and peace. The past is forgiven and forgotten. I am free in this moment.*
Slipped Disc	Feeling totally unsupported by life. Indecisive.	*Life supports all of my thoughts; therefore, I love and approve of myself, and all is well.*
Snoring	Stubborn refusal to let go of old patterns.	*I release all that is unlike love and joy in my mind. I move from the past into the new and fresh and vital.*
Spinal Meningitis	Extreme family discord. Living in an atmosphere of anger and fear. Lots of inner turmoil. Lack of support.	*I choose to create peace in my mind, my body and my world. All is well. I am safe and loved.*
Spine	Flexible support of life.	*I am supported by life.*

184

Spinal Curvature	The inability to flow with the support of life. Fear and trying to hold on to old ideas. Not trusting life. Lack of integrity. No courage of convictions.	I release all fears. I now trust the process of life. I know that life is for me. I stand straight and tall with love.
Spleen	Obsessions. Being obsessed about things.	I love and approve of myself. I trust the process of life to be there for me. I am safe. All is well.
Sprains	Anger and resistance. Not wanting to move in a certain direction in life.	I trust the process of life to take me only to my highest good. I am at peace.
Sterility	Fear and resistance to the process of life, OR not needing to go through the parenting experience.	I trust in the process of life. I am always in the right place, doing the right things, at the right time. I love and approve of myself.
Stiff Neck	Unbending bullheadedness.	It is safe to see other viewpoints.
Stiffness	Rigid, stiff thinking.	I am safe enough to be flexible in my mind.
Stomach	Holds nourishment. Digests ideas.	I digest life with ease.
- Problems	Dread. Fear of the new. Inability to assimilate the new.	Life agrees with me. I assimilate the new every moment of every day. All is well.

Stroke	Giving up. Resistance. Rather die than change. Rejection of life.	Life is change, and I adapt easily to the new. I accept life — past, present and future.
Stuttering	Insecurity. Lack of self-expression. Not being allowed to cry.	I am free to speak up for myself. I am now secure in my own expression. I communicate only with love.
Swelling	Being stuck in thinking. Clogged, painful ideas.	My thoughts flow freely and easily. I move through ideas with ease.
Syphilis	See Venereal Disease	I decide to be me. I approve of myself as I am.
Tapeworm	Strong belief in being a victim and unclean. Helpless to the seeming attitudes of others.	Others only reflect the good feelings I have about myself. I love and approve of all that I am.
Teeth	Represent decisions.	
- Problems	Longstanding indecisiveness. Inability to break down ideas for analysis and decisions.	I make my decisions based on the principles of truth, and I rest securely knowing that only Right Action is taking place in my life.
Testicles	Masculine principle, masculinity.	It is safe to be a man.
Tetanus	A need to release angry, festering thoughts.	I allow the love from my own heart to wash through me and cleanse and heal every part of my body and my emotions.

Throat	Avenue of expression. Channel of creativity.	*I open my heart and sing the joys of love.*
– Problems	The inability to speak up for one's self. Swallowed anger. Stifled creativity. Refusal to change.	*It's okay to make noise. I express myself freely and joyously. I speak up for myself with ease. I express my creativity. I am willing to change.*
Thymus	Master gland of the immune system. Feeling attacked by life. "They" are out to get me.	*My loving thoughts keep my immune system strong. I am safe inside and out. I heal myself with love.*
Thyroid	Humiliation. I never get to do what I want to do. When is it going to be my turn?	*I move beyond old limitations and now allow myself to express freely and creatively.*
Tinnitus	Refusal to listen. Not hearing the inner voice. Stubbornness.	*I trust my Higher Self. I listen with love to my inner voice. I release all that is unlike the action of love.*
Toes	Represent the minor details of the future.	*All details take care of themselves.*
Tonsillitis	Fear. Repressed emotions. Stifled creativity.	*My good now flows freely. Divine ideas express through me. I am at peace.*

Tuberculosis	Wasting away from selfishness. Possessive. Cruel thoughts. Revenge.	*As I love and approve of myself, I create a joyful, peaceful world to live in.*
Tumors	Nursing old hurts and shocks. Building remorse.	*I lovingly release the past and turn my attention to this new day. All is well.*
Ulcers	Fear. A strong belief that you are not good enough. What is eating away at you?	*I love and approve of myself. I am at peace. I am calm. All is well.*
Urinary Infections	"Pissed off." Usually at the opposite sex or a lover. Blaming others.	*I release the pattern in my consciousness that created this condition. I am willing to change. I love and approve of myself.*
Uterus	Represents the home of creativity.	*I am at home in my body.*
Vaginitis	Anger at a mate. Sexual guilt. Punishing the self.	*Others mirror the love and self-approval I have for myself. I rejoice in my sexuality.*
Varicose Veins	Standing in a situation you hate. Discouragement. Feeling overworked and overburdened.	*I stand in truth and live and move in joy. I love life, and I circulate freely.*
Venereal Disease	Sexual guilt. Need for punishment. Belief that the genitals are sinful or dirty. Abusing another.	*I lovingly and joyously accept my sexuality and its expression. I accept only thoughts that support me and make me feel good.*

Vitiligo	Not belonging. Feeling completely outside of things. Not one of the group.	*I am at the very center of life, and I am totally connected in love.*
Vulva	Represents vulnerability.	*It is safe to be vulnerable.*
Warts	Little expressions of hate. Belief in ugliness.	*I am the love and the beauty of life in full expression.*
Wisdom Tooth Impacted	Not giving mental space to create a firm foundation.	*I open my consciousness to the expansion of life. There is plenty of space for me to grow and to change.*
Wrist	Represents movement and ease.	*I handle all my experiences with wisdom, with love, and with ease.*

In the infinity of life where I am,
all is perfect, whole and complete.
I accept perfect health as the natural state of my being.
I now consciously release any mental patterns within me
that could express as dis-ease in any way.
I love and approve of myself.
I love and approve of my body.
I feed it nourishing foods and beverages.
I exercise it in ways that are fun.
I recognize my body as a wonderous and magnificent machine,
and I feel privileged to live in it.
I love lots of energy.
All is well in my world.

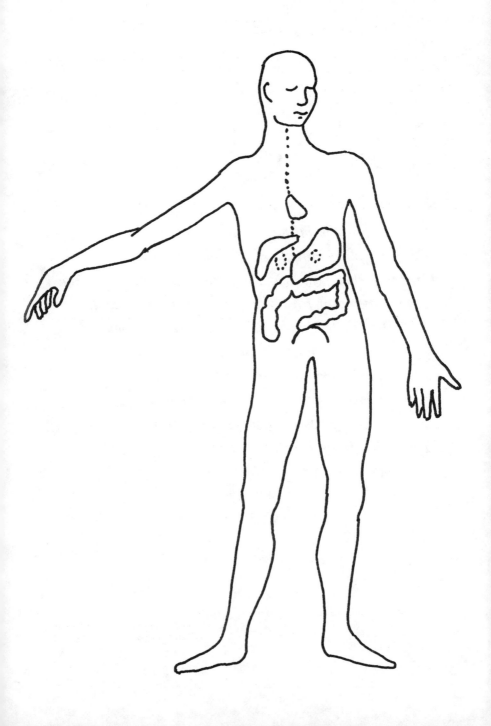

NEW THOUGHT PATTERNS

FACE: (Acne): I love and accept myself where I am right now. I am wonderful.

SINUSES: I am one with all of life. No one has the power to irritate me unless I allow it. Peace, harmony. I deny any beliefs in calendars.

EYES: I am free. I look ahead freely because life is eternal and filled with joy. I see with loving eyes. No one can ever hurt me.

THROAT: I can speak up for myself. I express myself freely. I am creative. I speak with love.

LUNGS: The breath of life flows easily through me. (Bronchitis): Peace. No one can irritate me. (Asthma): I am free to take charge of my life.

HEART: Joy, love, peace. I joyfully accept life.

LIVER: I let go of everything which I no longer need. My consciousness is now cleansed and my concepts are fresh, new and vital.

LARGE INTESTINE: I am free; I release the past. Life flows easily through me. (Hemorrhoids): I release all pressure and burdens. I live in the joyous present.

GENITALS: (Impotence): Power. I allow the full potential of my sexual principle to operate with ease and joy. I lovingly and joyously accept my sexuality. There is no guilt and no punishment.

KNEE: Forgiveness, tolerance, compassion. I move forward without hesitation.

SKIN: I get attention in positive ways. I am secure. No one threatens my individuality. I am at peace. The world is safe and friendly. I release all anger and resentment. Whatever I need will always be here. I accept my good without guilt. I am peaceful with all the little things in life.

BACK: Life itself supports me. I trust the universe. I freely give love and trust. Lower back: I trust the universe. I am courageous and independent.

BRAIN: All of life is change. My growth patterns are ever new.

HEAD: Peace, love, joy, relaxation. I relax into the flow of life and let life flow through me with ease.

EARS: I listen to God. I hear the joys of life. I am part of life. I listen with love.

MOUTH: I am a decisive person. I follow through. I welcome new ideas and new concepts.

NECK: I am flexible. I welcome other viewpoints.

SHOULDERS: (Bursitis): I release anger in harmless ways. Love releases and relaxes. Life is joyous and free; all that I accept is good.

HANDS: I handle all ideas with love and ease.

FINGERS: I relax knowing the wisdom of life takes care of all details.

STOMACH: I assimilate new ideas easily. Life agrees with me; nothing can irritate me. I am calm.

KIDNEYS: I seek only good everywhere. Right action is taking place. I am fulfilled.

BLADDER: I release the old and welcome the new.

PELVIS: (Vaginitis): Forms and channels may change but love is never lost. (Menstrual): I am balanced in all changes of cycles. I bless my body with love. All parts of my body are beautiful.

HIP: I joyfully move forward supported and sustained by the power of life. I move into my greater good. I am secure. (Arthritis): Love. Forgiveness. I let others be themselves and I am free.

GLANDS: I am in total balance. My system is in order. I love life and circulate freely.

FEET: I stand in truth. I move forward with joy. I have spiritual understanding.

New thought patterns (positive affirmations) can heal and relax your body.

This diagram was made by Meganne Forbes using Louise L. Hay's book, *Heal Your Body*, Published by Louise L. Hay, 1979, New York.

Part 4

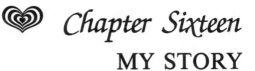 *Chapter Sixteen*
MY STORY

"We are all one."

"Will you tell me a little about your childhood, briefly." This is a question I have asked so many clients. It's not that I need to hear all the details, but I want to get a general pattern of where they are coming from. If they have problems now, the patterns that created them began a long time ago.

When I was a little girl of 18 months, I experienced my parents divorcing. I don't remember that as being so bad. What I do remember with horror is when my mother went to work as a live-in domestic and boarded me out. The story goes that I cried nonstop for three weeks. The people taking care of me couldn't handle that, and my mother was forced to take me back and make other arrangements. How she managed as a single parent brings my admiration today. Then, however, all I knew and cared about was that I was not getting all the loving attention I once had.

I have never been able to determine if my mother loved my stepfather or whether she just married him in order to provide a home for us. But it was not a good move. This man had been brought up in Europe in a heavy Germanic home with much brutality, and he had never learned any other way to manage a family. My mother became pregnant with my sister, and then the 1930's depression descended upon us, and we found ourselves stuck in a home of violence. I was five years old.

To add to the scenario, it was just about this time that a neighbor, an old wino, as I remember it, raped me. The doctor's examination is still vivid in my mind, as was the court case in which I was the star witness. The man was sentenced to 15 years in prison. I was told repeatedly that, "It was your fault," so I spent many years fearing that when he was released he would come and get me for being so terrible as to put him in jail.

Most of my childhood was spent enduring both physical and sexual abuse, with a lot of hard labor thrown in. My self-image became lower and lower, and few things seemed to go right for me. I began to express this pattern in the outside world.

There was an incident in the fourth grade that was so typical of what my life was like. We were having a party at school one day, and there were several cakes to share. Most of the children in this school except for me were from comfortable middle-class families. I was poorly dressed, with a funny bowl haircut, high topped black shoes, and I smelled from the raw garlic I had to eat every day to "keep the worms away." We never had cake. We couldn't afford it. There was an old neighbor woman who gave me 10¢ every week, and a dollar on my birthday and at Christmas. The 10¢ went into the family budget, and the dollar bought my underwear for the year at the dime store.

So this day we were having the party at school, and there was so much cake that as they were cutting it, some of the kids who could have cake almost every day were getting two and three pieces. When the teacher finally got around to me, (and of course I was last), there was no cake left. Not one piece.

I see clearly now that it was my "already confirmed belief" that I was worthless and did not *DESERVE* anything that put me at the end of the line with no cake. It was *MY* pattern. *THEY* were only being a mirror for my beliefs.

When I was 15, I could not take the sexual abuse any longer, and I ran away from home and from school. The job I found as a waitress in a diner seemed so much easier than the heavy yard work I had to do at home.

Being starved for love and affection and having the lowest of self-esteem, I willingly gave my body to whoever was kind to me; and just after my 16th birthday, I gave birth to a baby girl. I felt it was impossible to keep her; however, I was able to find her a good, loving home. I found a childless couple who longed for a baby. I lived in their home for the last four months, and when I went to the hospital, I had the child in their name.

Under such circumstances, I never experienced the joys of motherhood, only the loss and guilt and shame. Then it was only a shameful time to get over with as soon as possible. I only remember her big toes, which were unusual like mine. If we ever meet, I will know for sure if I see her toes. I left when the child was five days old.

I immediately went back home and said to my mother who had continued to be a victim, "Come on, you don't have to take this any longer. I'm getting you out of here." She came with me, leaving my ten-year-old sister, who had always been daddy's darling, to stay with her father.

After helping my mother get a job as a domestic in a small hotel and settling her into an apartment where she was free and comfortable, I felt my obligations were over. I left for Chicago with a girl friend to stay a month — and did not return for over 30 years.

In those early days, the violence I experienced as a child, combined with the sense of worthlessness I developed along the way, attracted men into my life who mistreated me and often beat me. I could have spent the rest of my life berating men, and I probably would still be having the same experiences. Gradually, however, through positive work experiences, my self-esteem grew and those kinds of men began to leave my life. They no longer fit my old pattern of unconsciously believing I deserved abuse. I do not condone their behavior, but if it were not "my pattern," they would not have been attracted to me. Now, a man who abuses women does not even know I exist. Our patterns no longer attract.

After a few years in Chicago doing rather menial work, I went to New York and was lucky enough to become a high fashion model. Yet even modeling for the big designers did not help my self-esteem very much. It only gave me more ways to find fault with myself. I refused to recognize my own beauty.

I was in the fashion industry for many years. I met and married a wonderful, educated English gentleman. We traveled the world, met royalty and even had dinner at the White House. Though I was a model and had a wonderful man, still my self-esteem remained low until years later when I began the inner work.

One day after 14 years of marriage, he announced his desire to marry another, just when I was beginning to believe that good things can last. Yes, I was crushed. But time passes, and I lived on. I could feel my life changing, and a numerologist one spring confirmed it by telling me that in the fall a small event would occur that would change my life.

It was so small that I didn't notice it until several months later. Quite by chance, I had gone to a meeting at the Church of Religious Science in New York City. While their message was new to me, something within me said, "Pay attention," and so I did. I went not only to the Sunday services, but I began to take their weekly classes. The beauty and fashion world was losing its interest to me. How many years could I remain concerned with my waist measurement or the shape of my eyebrows? From a high school dropout who never studied anything, I now became an avaricious student devouring everything I could lay my hands on that pertained to metaphysics and healing.

The Church of Religious Science became a new home for me. Even though most of my life was going on as usual, this new course of study began to take up more and more of my time. The next thing I knew, it was three years later, and I was eligible to apply to become one of the Church's licensed practitioners. I passed the test, and that's where I began, as a church counselor, many years ago.

It was a small beginning. During this time I became a Transcendental Meditator. My church was not giving the Ministerial Training Program for another year, so I decided to do something special for myself. I went to college for six months — MIU, Maharishis' International University — in Fairfield, Iowa.

It was the perfect place for me at that time. In the freshman year, every Monday morning we began a new subject, things I had only heard of, such as biology, chemistry, and even the theory of relativity. Every Saturday morning there was a test. Sunday was free, and Monday morning we began anew.

There were none of the distractions so typical of my life in New York City. After dinner we all went to our rooms to study. I was the oldest kid on campus and loved every moment of it. No smoking, drinking or drugs were allowed, and we meditated four times a day. The day I left, I thought I would collapse from the cigarette smoke in the airport.

Back to New York I went to resume my life. Soon I began taking the Ministerial Training Program. I became very active in the church and in its social activities. I began speaking at their noon meetings and seeing clients. This quickly blossomed into a full time career. Out of the work I was doing, I was inspired to put together the little book *HEAL YOUR BODY,* which began as a simple list of metaphysical causations for physical illnesses in the body. I began to lecture and travel and hold small classes.

Then one day I was diagnosed as having cancer.

With my background of being raped at five and having been a battered child, it was no wonder I manifested cancer in the vaginal area.

Like anyone else who has just been told they have cancer, I went into total panic. Yet because of all my work with clients, I knew that mental healing worked, and here I was being given a chance to prove it to myself. After all, I had written the book on mental patterns, and I knew cancer is a disease of deep resentment that has been held for a long time until it literally eats away at the body. I had been refusing to be willing to dissolve all the anger and resentment at "them" over my childhood. There was no time to waste, I had a lot of work to do.

The word *INCURABLE,* which is so frightening to so many people, means to me that this particular condition cannot be cured by any outer means and that we must go within to find the cure. If I had an operation to get rid of the cancer and did not clear the mental pattern that created it, then the doctors would just keep cutting Louise until there was no more Louise to cut. I didn't like that idea.

If I had the operation to remove the cancerous growth and also cleared the mental pattern that was causing the cancer, then it would not return. If cancer or any other illness returns, I do not believe it is because they did not "get it all out," but rather that the patient has made no mental changes. He or she just recreates the same illness, perhaps in a different part of the body.

I also believed that if I could clear the mental pattern that created this cancer, then I would not even need the operation. So I bargained for time, and the doctors grudgingly gave me three months when I said I did not have the money.

I immediately took responsibility for my own healing. I read and investigated everything I could find on alternative ways to assist my healing process.

I went to several health food stores and bought every book they had on the subject of cancer. I went to the library and did more reading. I checked out foot reflexology and colon therapy and thought they both would be beneficial to me. I seemed to be led to exactly the right people. After reading about foot reflexology, I wanted to find a practitioner. I attended a lecture, and while I usually sit in the front row, this night I was compelled to sit in the back. Within a minute a man came and sat beside me and — guess what? He was a foot reflexologist who visited the home. He came to me three times a week for two months and was a great help.

I knew I also had to love myself a great deal more than I was. There was little love expressed in my childhood, and no one had made it okay for me to feel good about myself. I had adopted their attitudes of continually picking on and criticizing me, which had become second nature.

I had come to the realization through my work with the Church that it was okay and even essential for me to love and approve of myself. Yet I kept putting it off — rather like the diet you will always start tomorrow. But I could no longer put it off. At first it was very difficult for me to do things like stand in front of the mirror and say things like, "Louise, I love you. I really love you."

However, as I persisted, I found that several situations came up in my life where in the past I would have berated myself and now, because of the mirror exercise and other work, I was not doing so. I was making some progress.

I knew I had to clear the patterns of resentment I had been holding since childhood. It was imperative for me to let go of the blame.

Yes, I had had a very difficult childhood with a lot of abuse — mental, physical and sexual. But that was many years ago, and it was no excuse for the way I was treating myself now. I was literally eating my body with cancerous growth because I had not forgiven.

It was time for me to go beyond the incidents themselves and to begin to *UNDERSTAND* what types of experiences could have created people who would treat a child that way.

With the help of a good therapist, I expressed all the old, bottled-up anger by beating pillows and howling with rage. This made me feel cleaner. Then I began to piece together the scraps of stories my parents had told me of their own childhoods. I started to see a larger picture of their lives. With my growing understanding, and from an adult viewpoint, I began to have compassion for their pain; and the blame slowly began to dissolve.

In addition, I hunted for a good nutritionist to help me cleanse and detoxify my body from all the junky foods I had eaten over the years. I learned that junky foods accumulate and create a toxic body. Junky thoughts accumulate and create toxic conditions in the mind. I was given a very strict diet with lots of green vegetables and not much else. I even had colonics three times a week for the first month.

I did not have an operation — however, as a result of all the thorough mental and physical cleansing, six months after my diagnosis I was able to get the medical profession to agree with what I already knew — that I no longer had even a trace of cancer! Now I knew from personal experience that *DISEASE CAN BE HEALED, IF WE ARE WILLING TO CHANGE THE WAY WE THINK AND BELIEVE AND ACT!*

Sometimes what seems to be a big tragedy turns out to become the greatest good in our lives. I learned so much from that experience, and I came to value life in a new way. I began to look at what was really important to me, and I made a decision finally to leave the treeless city of New York and its extreme weather. Some of my clients insisted they would "die" if I left them, and I assured them I would be back twice a year to check on their progress, and telephones can reach everywhere. So I closed my business and took a leisurely train trip to California, deciding to use Los Angeles as a starting point.

Even though I had been born here many years before, I knew almost no one any more except for my mother and sister, who both now lived on the outskirts about an hour away. We had never been a close family nor an open one, but still I was unpleasantly surprised to learn that my mother had been blind for a few years and no one had bothered to tell me. My sister was too "busyish" to see me, so I let her be and began to set up my new life.

My little book *HEAL YOUR BODY* opened many doors for me. I began to go to every New Age type of meeting I could find. I would introduce myself, and when appropriate, give out a copy of the little book. For the first six months I went to the beach a lot, knowing that when I became busy there would be less time for such leisurely pursuits. Slowly the clients appeared. I was asked to speak here and there, and things began to come together as Los Angeles welcomed me. Within a couple of years, I was able to move into a lovely home.

My new lifestyle in Los Angeles was a large jump in consciousness from my early upbringing. Things were going smoothly, indeed. How swiftly our lives can change completely.

One night I received a phone call from my sister, the first call in two years. She told me our mother, now 90, blind and almost deaf, had fallen and broken her back. In one moment my mother went from being a strong, independent woman to being a helpless child in pain.

She broke her back and also broke open the wall of secrecy around my sister. Finally we were all beginning to communicate. I discovered that my sister also had a severe back problem that impaired her sitting and walking and which was very painful. She suffered in silence, and though she looked anorexic, her husband did not know she was ill.

After spending a month in the hospital, my mother was ready to go home. But in no way could she take care of herself, so she came to live with me.

Though trusting in the process of life, I did not know how I could handle it all, so I said to God, "Okay, I will take care of her but you have to give me help, and you have to provide the money!"

It was quite an adjustment for both of us. She arrived on a Saturday; and the following Friday, I had to go to San Francisco for four days. I could not leave her alone, and I had to go. I said, "God, you handle this. I have to have the right person to help us before I leave."

On the following Thursday, the perfect person had "appeared," and moved in to organize my home for my mother and me. It was another confirmation of one of my basic beliefs, "Whatever I need to know is revealed to me and whatever I need comes to me in Divine right order."

I realized it was lesson time for me once again. Here was an opportunity to clean up a lot of that garbage from childhood.

My mother had not been able to protect me when I was a child; however, I could and would take care of her now. Between my mother and my sister, a new whole adventure began.

To give my sister the help she asked for presented another challenge. I learned that when I had rescued my mother so many years ago, my stepfather then turned his rage and pain against my sister, and it was her turn to be brutalized.

I realized that what started out to be a physical problem was then greatly exaggerated by fear and tension, plus the belief that no one could help her. So here was Louise, not wanting to be a rescuer and yet wanting to give her sister an opportunity to choose wellness at this point in her life.

Slowly the unraveling began, and it's still going on. We progress step by step as I strive to provide an atmosphere of safety while we explore various alternative avenues of healing.

My mother, on the other hand, responds very well. She exercises as best she can four times a day. Her body gets stronger and more flexible. I took her to get a hearing aid, and she became more interested in life. In spite of her Christian Science beliefs, I persuaded her to have a cataract removed from one eye. What a joy for her to begin to see again and for us to see the world through her eyes. She is so pleased to read again.

My mother and I began to find time to sit and talk to each other in ways we had never done before. A new understanding developed between us. Today, we both become freer as we cry and laugh and hug together. Sometimes she pushes my buttons, which only tells me there is something further for me to clear. This is where my life is now in the autumn of 1984.

*   *   *

My mother left the planet peacefully in 1985. I miss her and love her. We completed all we could together, and now we are both free.

My work continues on an ever-expanding level. I no longer see private clients as I now devote my time to traveling and lecturing around the world. My staff has increased considerably. The Hay Institute lovingly oversees our workshops and seminars which now include a number of other personally trained teachers. I have drawn in and trained people whose beliefs resonate with mine. Combining our diverse backgrounds and life experiences has added to the richness of what we have to offer. And the Wednesday night AIDS Support Group, The Hayride, that began four and a half years ago still meets in the Los Angeles area. It now draws up to 800 people every week.

In the infinity of life where I am,
all is perfect, whole and complete.
Each one of us, myself included, experiences the richness
and fullness of life in ways that are meaningful to us.
I now look at the past with love and choose
to learn from my old experiences.
There is no right or wrong, nor good or bad.
The past is over and done.
There is only the experience of the moment.
I love myself for bringing myself
through this past into this present moment.
I share what and who I am,
for I know we are all one in Spirit.
All is well in my world.

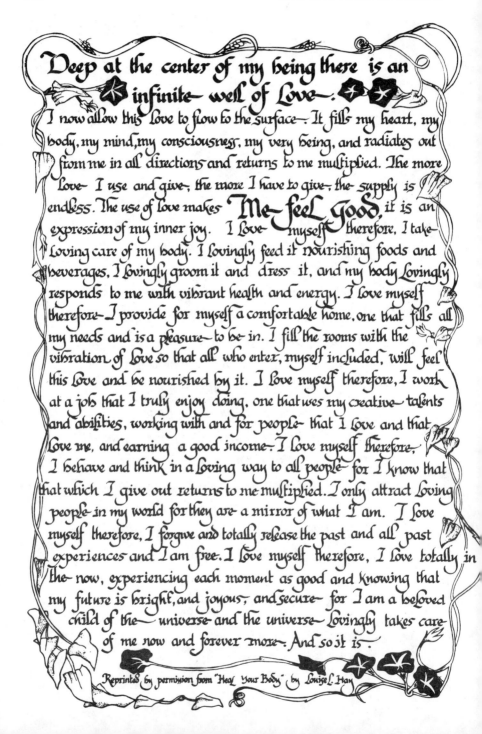

Deep at the center of my being there is an infinite well of Love.

I now allow this love to flow to the surface. It fills my heart, my body, my mind, my consciousness, my very being, and radiates out from me in all directions and returns to me multiplied. The more Love I use and give, the more I have to give, the supply is endless. The use of love makes **Me feel good,** it is an expression of my inner joy. I Love myself therefore, I take Loving care of my body. I lovingly feed it nourishing foods and beverages, I lovingly groom it and dress it, and my body lovingly responds to me with vibrant health and energy. I love myself therefore I provide for myself a comfortable home, one that fills all my needs and is a pleasure to be in. I fill the rooms with the vibration of love so that all who enter, myself included, will feel this love and be nourished by it. I love myself therefore, I work at a job that I truly enjoy doing, one that uses my creative talents and abilities, working with and for people that I love and that love me, and earning a good income. I love myself therefore, I behave and think in a loving way to all people for I know that that which I give out returns to me multiplied. I only attract loving people in my world for they are a mirror of what I am. I love myself therefore, I forgive and totally release the past and all past experiences and I am free. I love myself therefore, I love totally in the now, experiencing each moment as good and knowing that my future is bright, and joyous, and secure for I am a beloved child of the universe and the universe lovingly takes care of me now and forever more. And so it is.

Reprinted by permission from "Heal Your Body" by Louise L. Hay

Holistic Healing Recommendations

BODY

Nutrition
Diet, Food Combining, Macro-Biotic,
Natural Herbs, Vitamins, Bach Flower Remedies,
Homeopathy.

Exercise
Yoga, Trampoline, Walking, Dance, Cycling,
Tai-Chi, Martial Arts, Swimming, Sports, Etc.

Alternative Therapies
Acupuncture, Acupressure, Colon Therapy,
Reflexology, Radionics, Chromotherapy,
Massage & Body Work
Alexander, Bioenergenics, Touch for Health,
Feldenkrais, Deep Tissue Work, Rolfing,
Polarity, Trager, Reiki.

Relaxation Techniques
Systematic Desensitization, Deep Breathing,
Biofeedback, Sauna, Water Therapy (Hot Tub),
Slant Board, Music.

Books
Getting Well Again - Simonton
Herbally Yours - Royal
How to Get Well - Airola
Food Is Your Best Medicine - Bieler
I Love My Body - Hay

MIND

Affirmations, Mental Imagery, Guided Imagery,
Meditation, Loving the Self.

Psychologial Techniques
Gestalt, Hypnosis, NLP, Focusing, T.A., Rebirthing,
Dream Work, Psycho Drama, Past Life Regression,
Jung, Humanistic Psychotherapies, Astrology,
Art Therapy.

Groups
Insight, est, Loving Relationship Training,
ARAS, Ken Keyes Groups, All 12-Step Programs,
Aids Project, Rebirthing.

Books
Creative Visualization - Gawain
Visualization - Bry
Focusing - Gendlin
The Power of Affirmations - Fankhauser
Superbeings - Price
Love is Letting Go of Fear - Jampolsky
Teach Only Love - Jampolsky
A Conscious Person's Guide to Relationships - Keyes
Moneylove - Gillies
Loving Relationships - Ray
Celebration of Breath - Ray
Heal Your Body - Hay

SPIRIT

Prayer
>Asking for What You Want, Forgiveness,
>Receiving (Allowing the Presence of God to Enter),
>Accepting, Surrendering.

Spiritual Group Work
>M.S.I.A., T.M., Siddah Foundation,
>Self Realization, Religious Science,
>Unity.

Books
>*Course in Miracles* - Foundation for Inner Peace
>*Autobiography of a Yogi* - Yogananda
>Any book by Emmett Fox
>*The Nature of Personal Reality-* Roberts
>*Your Needs Met* - Addington
>*The Manifestation Process* - Price
>*The Science of Mind* - Holmes

I have long believed: "Everything I need to know is revealed to me." "Everything I need comes to me." "All is well in my life." There is no new knowledge. All is ancient and infinite. It is my joy and pleasure to gather together wisdom and knowledge for the benefit of those on the healing pathway. I dedicate this offering to all of you who have taught me what I know: to my many clients, to my friends in the field, to my teachers, and to the Divine Infinite Intelligence for channeling through me that which others need to hear.

Louise L. Hay

INDEX

cont.

BOOKS AND AUDIO TAPES BY LOUISE L. HAY

Books

The AIDS Book: Creating A Positive Approach
Colors & Numbers
Heal Your Body
Heart Thoughts: A Treasury of Inner Wisdom
A Garden of Thoughts: My Affirmation Journal
Love Your Body
Love Yourself, Heal Your Life Workbook
The Power is Within You

Coloring Books/Audios for Children

Lulu and the Ant: A Message of Love
Lulu and the Dark: Conquering Fears
Lulu and Willy the Duck: Learning Mirror Work

Audio Tapes

AIDS: A Positive Approach
Cancer: Discovering Your Healing Power
Feeling Fine Affirmations
Gift of the Present with Joshua Leeds
Heal Your Body Book on Tape
Love Your Body Book on Tape
Loving Yourself
Morning and Evening Meditations
Self Healing
Songs of Affirmation with Joshua Leeds
What I Believe/Deep Relaxation
You Can Heal Your Life Study Course
You Can Heal Your Life Book on Tape

Conversations on Living Lecture Series

Change and Transition
Dissolving Barriers
The Forgotten Child Within
How to Love Yourself
The Power of Your Spoken Word
Receiving Prosperity
Totality of Possibilities
Your Thoughts Create Your Life

Personal Power Through Imagery Series

Anger Releasing
Forgiveness/Loving the Inner Child

Subliminal Mastery Series

Feeling Fine Affirmations
Love Your Body Affirmations
Safe Driving Affirmations
Self-Esteem Affirmations
Self-Healing Affirmations
Stress-Free Affirmations